User's Guide

Microsoft® PowerPoint®

The Most Popular Presentation Graphics Program
Version 4.0

For Apple® Macintosh Series or Windows™ Series

Microsoft Corporation

Contents

Contents vi

Before You Begin

The *Microsoft® PowerPoint® User's Guide* contains detailed information about using the PowerPoint presentation graphics program for the Windows™ operating system and PowerPoint for Macintosh®. When instructions for the two versions of PowerPoint differ, you'll see a note such as "(Windows)" or "(Macintosh)."

Microsoft PowerPoint Documentation

To help you learn PowerPoint and produce effective and attractive presentations, the printed documentation and online Help include the following features.

Quick steps for creating a presentation In Chapter 1, "An Overview of PowerPoint," you'll find out how easy it is to make a PowerPoint presentation. Just follow along on your computer while we lead you through the quick steps for creating a presentation.

Online Help The online documentation includes:

- Step-by-step instructions on how to use PowerPoint.
- "Nuts and bolts" descriptions of common procedures that stay on your screen as you work.
- In-depth procedures not covered in the printed documentation.
- PowerPoint concepts and terms to acquaint you with the PowerPoint vocabulary.
- A synopsis of what's new in PowerPoint 4.0.

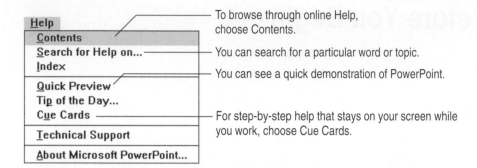

Back cover and appendix The back cover and the appendixes of the *User's Guide* provide handy reference information about shortcuts, sample templates, the PowerPoint tools and toolbars, and using PowerPoint on a network.

Installing PowerPoint

Before getting to work, you need to install Microsoft PowerPoint on your computer. The PowerPoint Setup program does this for you. You can choose one of four kinds of installation: a complete installation, a typical installation that loads PowerPoint and its most commonly used components, a custom installation that allows you to select just those components you want, or a minimal installation especially for laptop computer users.

To take full advantage of PowerPoint, we suggest you install the complete version of the program. Of course, you can always add or remove parts of PowerPoint at any time. For more information about installation options, see Appendix B, "Detailed Information About Installing PowerPoint 4.0."

Be sure to send in your registration card. Only registered owners receive Microsoft's total product support, including early notification of upgrades.

Copying PowerPoint and the PowerPoint Disks

Before you install PowerPoint on your hard disk, you may want to copy the program disks as a backup. You can copy the PowerPoint program disks for your own use, but be aware that the Microsoft PowerPoint license prohibits making more than one backup copy. Your license lets you install PowerPoint on another computer, such as a laptop or a home computer, provided that you use only one copy of PowerPoint at a time and that you are the primary user where the software is installed most of the time. For more information, read your Microsoft PowerPoint license.

As part of the PowerPoint package, you get the PowerPoint Viewer, which allows you to show your presentations on computers that don't have PowerPoint installed. The Viewer comes on its own disk, and you can copy it and share it with others so they can see PowerPoint presentations on their computers.

How to Install PowerPoint for Windows

Minimum System Requirements

- Microsoft MS-DOS® operating system version 3.1 or later (MS-DOS version 5.0 or later recommended)
- Microsoft Windows™ operating system version 3.1 or later (must be acquired separately)
- Personal computer using 80386 or higher microprocessor
- Minimum 4 MB of memory
- Hard disk
- 3.5-inch high-density (1.44 MB) disk drive
- VGA, EGA, XGA, or any video adapter supported by Microsoft Windows version 3.1 or later (except CGA) (256-color video adapter and compatible Microsoft Windows version 3.1 driver recommended)
- Microsoft Mouse or compatible pointing device

To print, choose from among all printers supported by Microsoft Windows version 3.1.

Optional Equipment

- Microsoft Windows Graphical Environment for Pen Computing
- Extra memory
- 256-color video adapter and compatible Windows version 3.1 driver
- Film recorder compatible with Windows version 3.1

▶ **To install PowerPoint on a PC**

Instructions for installing PowerPoint on a network are in Appendix A, "Using PowerPoint on a Network." Follow these instructions for installing PowerPoint locally on a single-user system.

Before you install PowerPoint for Windows, you must have MS-DOS and Microsoft Windows installed on your computer. For information about installing Windows, see your Windows documentation.

1. Close any open applications on your computer, make sure Windows is running, and then go to the Program Manager.

2. Insert the disk labeled Disk 1 into drive A or drive B and close the drive door, if necessary.

3. From the Program Manager File menu, choose Run, and then type **A: setup** or **B: setup** (depending on the drive you are using) in the command-line box, and click OK.

4. Choose the installation option you want and provide the information requested in the Microsoft PowerPoint Setup dialog boxes. These include:

   ▪ Typing your name and your company name.

   ▪ Changing the directory or drive into which PowerPoint 4.0 will be installed. If you have PowerPoint 3.0 on your system and you don't want to replace it with the newer version, you must specify a separate directory for PowerPoint 4.0. Otherwise PowerPoint assumes you want to replace the older version.

   ▪ Specifying the kind of installation you want—Typical, Complete/Custom, or Laptop (Minimum).

     The Complete installation requires the most hard disk space, while the Typical and Laptop (Minimum) options require less space. For more information on each option, see Appendix B, "Detailed Information About Setting Up PowerPoint 4.0."

   ▪ Specifying the Program Manager group in which you want the PowerPoint icon placed.

5. Once installation begins, you'll be prompted to insert the PowerPoint installation disks.

How to Install PowerPoint for Macintosh

Minimum System Requirements

▪ System 7.0 or later

▪ Minimum 4 MB of memory

▪ Hard disk

▪ 3.5-inch (1.4 MB) drive

▪ Color monitor (video card if needed by your computer)

Optional Equipment

▪ QuickTime™ to play QuickTime movies

▪ Extra memory

▪ Film recorder compatible with Macintosh

▶ **To install PowerPoint on a Macintosh**

1. Restart your computer while holding down the SHIFT key as your Macintosh restarts to turn off all INITs.

   If you have virus protection software installed, make sure that it is deactivated. (You can drag your virus protection software out of your System Folder to another folder and then restart your computer.) If you are installing from a network, make sure the Chooser is closed before running the installer. Close any open applications.

2. Insert Disk 1 into your floppy drive.

3. Double-click the Setup icon.

4. Choose the options you want and provide the information requested in the Microsoft PowerPoint Setup dialog boxes. These include:

   ▪ Typing your name and your company name.

   ▪ Changing the folder or drive into which PowerPoint 4.0 will be installed.

     If you have PowerPoint 3.0 on your system and you don't want to replace it with the newer version, you must specify a separate location for PowerPoint 4.0. Otherwise PowerPoint will assume you want to replace the older version.

   ▪ Specifying the kind of installation you want—Typical, Complete/Custom, or Laptop (Minimum).

     The Complete installation requires the most hard disk space, while the Typical and Laptop (Minimum) options require less space. For more information on each option, see Appendix B, "Detailed Information About Setting Up PowerPoint 4.0."

5. Once installation begins, you'll be prompted to insert the PowerPoint installation disks.

How to Install the PowerPoint Viewer (Windows and Macintosh)

The PowerPoint Viewer comes on its own disk with its own installation program. Please be sure to close all Windows-based applications before installing the Viewer.

▶ **To install the PowerPoint Viewer (Windows)**

1. Insert the PowerPoint Viewer disk into the appropriate drive.

2. Type **A: setup** or **B: setup** (depending on which drive you're using).

   The PowerPoint Viewer Setup dialog box appears.

3. If you want to change the directory in which the Viewer will be installed, type its name in the Install To box. Otherwise PowerPoint will be installed in the directory named in the Install To box.

4. Choose the OK button.

▶ **To install the PowerPoint Viewer (Macintosh)**

1. Insert the PowerPoint Viewer disk into the appropriate drive.

2. Open the disk by double-clicking its icon, and then double-click the Viewer icon.

3. Specify the folder into which you want the Viewer installed.

4. Choose the OK button.

Typographical Conventions

Before you start using Microsoft PowerPoint, it's important to understand the terms and typographical conventions we use in the documentation.

General Conventions

For explanations of specialized terms used in this book, see Chapter 1, "An Overview of PowerPoint."

We use the following kinds of formatting in the text to identify special information:

Formatting convention	Type of information
Triangular bullet (▶)	Step-by-step procedures. You can use procedural information by using both the mouse and keyboard. To choose a command from a menu, you can use either the mouse or a keyboard shortcut.
SMALL CAPITAL LETTERS	Keys on the keyboard appear in small capital letters. For example, the Enter key (Windows) or the Return key (Macintosh) appear as ENTER or RETURN. When we ask you to press a combination of keys, you'll see them connected by a +. For example, SHIFT +TAB means to press the SHIFT and the TAB keys at the same time.
Capitalized words	Commands you choose from the menus or dialog boxes appear capitalized. For example, you choose the Pick A Look Wizard command from the Format menu. Also, tool and button names are capitalized. You use the Text tool to type text, and the Line Color tool to change the color of lines and borders.
Bold type	Text we ask you to type appears in bold.

Mouse Conventions

You can use either a single-button mouse or a multiple-button mouse with Microsoft PowerPoint.

- If you have a multiple-button mouse, the left mouse button is the one you'll use most of the time (unless you have the mouse configured differently). Any procedure that requires you to click the secondary button asks you to click "the right mouse button."

- If you have a single-button mouse, pressing the CTRL key while clicking the mouse button is the same as clicking the right mouse button.

- "Point" means to position the mouse pointer so the tip of the pointer rests on whatever you want to point at on the screen.

- "Click" means to press and then immediately release the mouse button without moving the mouse.

- "Double-click" means to press and immediately release the mouse button twice without moving the mouse.

- "Drag" means to hold down the mouse button while moving the pointer across the screen.

C H A P T E R   1

An Overview of PowerPoint

Microsoft
PowerPoint

Welcome to PowerPoint, the best-selling presentation graphics software package in the world. PowerPoint's innovative tools and easy approach can help you make professional-looking presentations quickly and easily. By using some of PowerPoint's new content-development, preparation, and rehearsal features, you can be more effective in getting your point across.

Whether you need quick overheads for a team briefing, slides for a sales meeting, or dazzling effects for an on-screen presentation, PowerPoint has it all. Prompts, tips, and Cue Cards help you learn the product quickly; wizards, templates, and AutoLayouts help you get right to work; and a complete set of easy-to-use tools assures you have everything you need to get your point across and share information with others.

With PowerPoint you can:

- Quickly create strong overhead, paper, 35mm slide, or on-screen presentations.
- Augment your presentations with speaker's notes, outline pages, and audience handouts.
- Apply the knowledge you've already gained in learning Microsoft Word or Microsoft Excel. (If you know how to use either of these applications, you already know how to do more than 100 things in PowerPoint!)
- Get started quickly using the Quick Preview.
- Use materials you have created in other Microsoft products, such as Microsoft Word and Microsoft Excel, in PowerPoint.

All the tools and components you need are at your command and in your control.

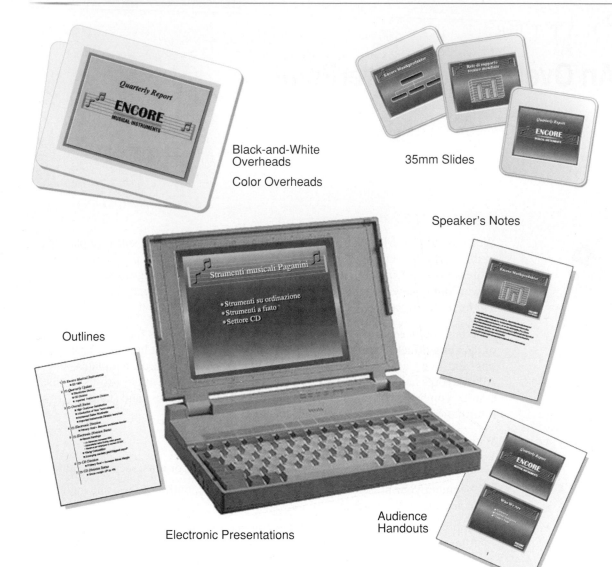

Black-and-White
Overheads

Color Overheads

35mm Slides

Speaker's Notes

Outlines

Electronic Presentations

Audience
Handouts

Microsoft
POWERPOINT

In This Chapter

What You'll Make with PowerPoint

PowerPoint is a complete presentation graphics package. It gives you everything you need to produce a professional-looking presentation—text handling, outlining, drawing, graphing, clip art, and so on. It also offers rich speaker support and aids to help you create truly effective presentations. PowerPoint makes you, the presenter, an independent producer of your own high-quality presentations. Now you can work on your own timetable.

Don't worry about consistency in design and color. PowerPoint can help you. If you don't consider yourself a designer, just apply one of the PowerPoint templates to your presentation. And choose from among the thousands of color schemes available. Whether you're making black-and-white overheads or putting together an electronic slide show, PowerPoint is easy to use.

Here's what you'll be making in PowerPoint:

Presentations

A PowerPoint presentation is a collection of your slides, handouts, speaker's notes, and your outline, all in one file. As you create slides, you're creating a presentation—you're designing how your presentation should look and giving it a format that carries through from beginning to end.

Slides

Slides are the individual "pages" of your presentation. Soon, you'll be creating slides with PowerPoint. Slides can have titles, text, graphs, drawn objects, shapes, clip art, drawn art, and visuals created with other applications—and more. You can print slides as black-and-white or color overhead transparencies or have 35mm slides made using a film or service bureau.

Handouts

To support your presentation, you have the option of providing handouts for your audience. Handouts consist of smaller, printed versions of your slides—either two, three, or six slides per page. If you want, you can print additional information such as your company name, the date, and the page number on each page.

Speaker's Notes

You can create and print speaker's notes. You'll see a small image of the slide on each notes page, along with any notes you type on the notes pages.

Outlines

As you're working on a presentation, you have the option of working with your presentation in outline form. In the outline, your titles and main text appear, but not your art or the text typed with the Text tool. You can print your outline, too.

How You'll Learn About PowerPoint

As a user of Microsoft PowerPoint, chances are you're also a user of Microsoft Word and Microsoft Excel. If so, you'll find lots of similarities among the three applications. We've worked for consistency in menus, commands, and dialog boxes. We've standardized toolbars so you don't have to rethink what the icons mean and how toolbars work whenever you switch between Microsoft applications. You can create something in PowerPoint and bring it into a Microsoft Word document. Or you can make a spreadsheet in Microsoft Excel and paste it into a PowerPoint presentation.

Quick Preview

The Quick Preview is a demonstration of PowerPoint features. It appears automatically when you start PowerPoint the first couple of times. It's also available to you on the Help menu, should you want to see it again or to show it to another user. The preview is designed to give you a quick overview of the main features of PowerPoint so you have a grasp of how the software works and what it can do for you.

▶ **To show the Quick Preview**

- From the Help menu, choose Quick Preview.

  The Quick Preview appears on your screen.

You'll find buttons at the bottom of the screen that you can use to pause the Quick Preview or to move forward and backward. You can watch as much as you want. To stop the Quick Preview before it's over, press ESC, and you'll return to PowerPoint.

The User's Guide

The printed guide describes how to use PowerPoint on the PC and on the Macintosh. It covers the PowerPoint basics for both platforms. When you need to use different procedures on the PC and on the Macintosh, both are described. The procedures you'll find on these pages will get you from point A to point B in the most straightforward manner. We introduce you to the quickest, simplest way to get things done.

Online Help

Help button

You can view the PowerPoint Help Contents window by choosing Contents from the Help menu. From this window, you can "jump" to more specific information.

Getting Help

You can get help in several ways. For example, you can use the Help button on the Standard toolbar to get context-sensitive help about items on the screen and commands. In addition, every dialog box and message window contains a Help button. To use the comprehensive online index, open the PowerPoint Help Contents window. To use other features in Help, use the Help command. You can even get help about how to use the Help system. Choose Contents from the Help menu. Then, in the Help window, choose How To Use Help from the Help menu.

Search: Having PowerPoint Look Up the Topic for You

The fastest way to get Help on a topic is to use the search feature. To open the Search dialog box, choose Search For Help On from the Help menu.

Index: Looking Up a Specific Topic

PowerPoint includes a comprehensive online index. To look up a topic in the Help index, choose Index from the Help menu, and then click the first letter of the topic you want to read about. You can also display the index by choosing the Index button in any Help topic.

Contents: Displaying Online Help Information

To see what's in Help, choose Contents from the Help menu in the PowerPoint window.

You can display step-by-step procedures while you're working in a document. To do this, choose Contents from the Help menu and, from the Contents window, choose Using PowerPoint. Scroll the screen to see the content covered in each Help chapter, and click the chapter you want. Then click the step-by-step procedure you want from that chapter. You can move or resize the Help topic window if it covers your document.

Context-Sensitive Help: Finding Out About Items on the Screen

To find out about an item on the screen, click the Help button on the Standard toolbar. When the pointer changes to a question mark, choose the command or click the window item on which you want help. PowerPoint displays the Help topic for the selected command or window item in the Help window.

Cue Cards

Cue Cards are procedures that stay on your screen while you work, giving you a brief step-by-step instruction on how to accomplish a task. Cue Cards cover common but sophisticated procedures such as adding a logo to every slide, creating "drill down" documents, or adding video to your slides.

▶ **To use Cue Cards**

1. From the Help menu, choose Cue Cards.

   The Cue Cards screen appears.

2. Click the topic or procedure you want help with.

   The Cue Cards lead you through the procedure step by step. Cue Cards stay on your screen until you close them.

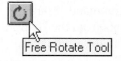

ToolTips and the Status Bar

When you position the pointer over one of the toolbar buttons, a yellow box appears telling you the name of the button. These boxes are called ToolTips. The status bar shows a longer description of the command while a ToolTip is displayed.

▶ **To turn ToolTips on or off**

1. From the View menu, choose Toolbars.

2. If the Show ToolTips check box is selected, clear the check box to turn ToolTips off.

   –or–

   If the Show ToolTips check box isn't selected, select the check box to turn ToolTips on.

   If you're a Macintosh user and Balloon Help is turned on, ToolTips are automatically off.

Balloon Help icon

Balloon Help (Macintosh)

▶ **To turn on Balloon Help**

1. From the Help menu, choose Show Balloons.
2. Point to the item on the screen for which you want help.

   If Balloon Help is available for that item, a balloon will appear.

Tip of the Day icon

Tip of the Day

Each time you start PowerPoint, you'll see a PowerPoint tip to help you use PowerPoint more effectively. You can view PowerPoint tips at any time by choosing the Tip Of The Day command from the Help menu. You can turn off the Tip of the Day by canceling the Show Tips At Startup check box in the Tip Of The Day dialog box.

Understanding the PowerPoint Window

The PowerPoint window, with its accompanying toolbars and menus, closely resembles the windows you work in for other Microsoft products, such as Microsoft Word and Microsoft Excel. Even if you're not familiar with Microsoft products, you'll find the PowerPoint window easy to understand and handy to use.

This section provides an overview of the major elements in the PowerPoint window, such as the status bar, scroll bar, and the toolbars.

The Main PowerPoint Window

The following illustration identifies each part of the PowerPoint window.

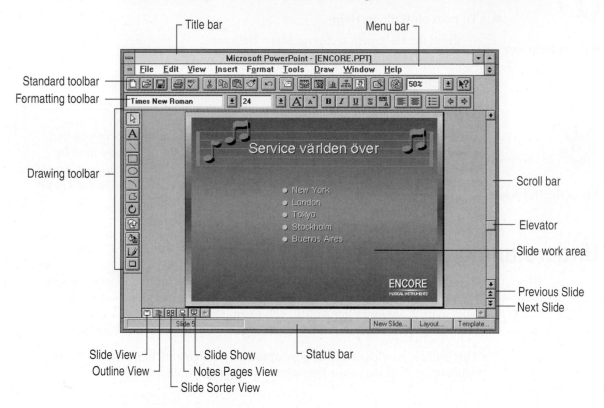

The Status Bar

Messages appear at the bottom of the window in an area called the status bar. These messages describe what you are seeing and doing in the PowerPoint window as you work. Normally, the status bar tells you which slide you're working on (Slide 1, Slide 2, and so on). When you choose a command, the status bar provides a short message telling you what that command will do.

Three shortcut buttons appear on the right side of the status bar—New Slide, Layout, and Template. Clicking the New Slide button presents the New Slide dialog box and adds a slide to your presentation immediately following the current slide using the slide layout you choose. Clicking the Layout button lets you change the layout of the current slide. Finally, clicking the Template button allows you to apply or change the template for your presentation.

The Scroll Bar

There's a vertical scroll bar on the right side of the PowerPoint window. The scroll bar has an elevator as well as double arrow buttons you can use to move from slide to slide.

▶ **To move to a particular slide using the scroll bar**

- Drag the elevator up or down to go to a particular slide.

    As you drag, the slide indicator box tells you what slide you're about to display. Release the mouse button when you reach the slide you're looking for.

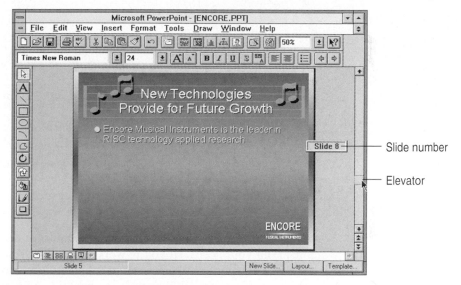

To move to a particular slide, drag the elevator until the slide number you want appears.

▶ **To move slide by slide using the double arrow buttons**

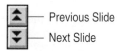
— Previous Slide
— Next Slide

You can quickly move one slide up or one slide down using the Previous Slide and Next Slide buttons below the vertical scroll bar.

- Click the double down arrows to go to the next slide. Click the double up arrows to go to the previous slide.

The Toolbars

You can use toolbars for quick access to commonly used commands and tools. When you first start PowerPoint and open a presentation, the Standard and Formatting toolbars are displayed just below the menu bar, and the Drawing toolbar is displayed vertically on the left side of the window. Different toolbars appear automatically in each view.

Standard toolbar

You can display as many of the toolbars as you want. Or you can choose to display none at all. Depending on your needs and the size of your monitor, you can add more toolbars to your work area. You can customize each toolbar by adding and removing buttons.

You can resize toolbars and drag them to different locations, arranging the window to suit your needs. (If you're working on a small screen, you can resize the toolbars manually to fit your workspace.) When you move toolbars and close PowerPoint, your changes will be there the next time you open PowerPoint.

You can customize toolbars by dragging unwanted buttons off and by dragging others onto the toolbars. You can put the same button on several toolbars. Buttons are always available in the Customize Toolbars dialog box, which is available when you choose the Customize command from the Tools menu.

You can also create a custom toolbar that includes just the buttons you use most often.

Displaying and hiding toolbars

▶ **To display or hide a toolbar on the screen**

1. From the View menu, choose Toolbars.

    The Toolbars dialog box appears.

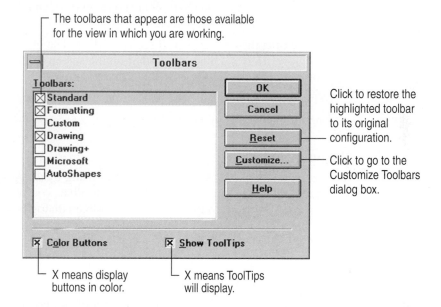

The toolbars that appear are those available for the view in which you are working.

Click to restore the highlighted toolbar to its original configuration.

Click to go to the Customize Toolbars dialog box.

X means display buttons in color.

X means ToolTips will display.

2. Click the box to the left of the toolbar name to select the toolbar or toolbars you want to display on-screen.

3. Choose OK.

    The toolbar you selected appears on the screen. You can move it to a different location if you want.

Tip You can hide toolbars you aren't using if your PowerPoint window becomes too cluttered.

Moving and resizing toolbars

You don't have to leave toolbars where they appear on the screen. You can place them wherever you want.

▶ **To move or resize a toolbar**

1. Click an open space on the toolbar (not a button), and drag the toolbar to a different location on the screen.

   As you drag the toolbar, you'll see its outline. The outline changes shape as you move from one place to another on the screen to show you how the toolbar will appear if you place it in that location.

2. When you find the right spot, release the mouse button.

   The toolbar moves to its new location.

Hiding toolbar buttons

You can hide toolbar buttons that you're not using by dragging them off the toolbars. When you remove a button from a toolbar, you're not deleting it—you're just returning it to the Customize Toolbars dialog box.

▶ **To hide a toolbar button**

1. From the Tools menu, choose Customize.

   The Customize Toolbars dialog box appears.

2. Drag the button you want to hide off the toolbar and drop it anywhere except on another toolbar.

   The button disappears.

Tip   You can hide a toolbar button or move it to another toolbar by holding down the ALT key (Windows) or the COMMAND key (Macintosh) and then dragging the button.

Adding buttons to toolbars

If you find you use a command often, you might want to set up the toolbars so they have precisely the buttons you want to use. Here's how you add buttons to toolbars.

▶ **To add a button to a toolbar**

1. From the Tools menu, choose Customize.

   The Customize Toolbars dialog box appears.

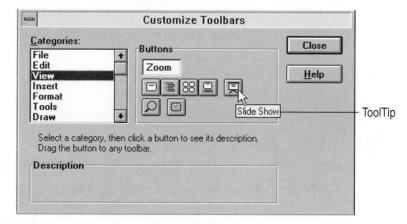

Pass the pointer over a button to find out its name.

2. In the Categories box, select a tool category that includes the button you want to add.

   The buttons in the category appear on the right.

   A scroll bar appears on the right when there are more buttons in the selected category than the window will hold.

3. When you find the button you want to add, drag it and drop it on the toolbar where you want it.

   You can drag and drop as many buttons as you want.

4. When you finish adding buttons to toolbars, choose the Close button in the Customize Toolbars dialog box.

   You can now move the toolbar and change its shape if you want.

Tip   You can drag buttons from one toolbar to another or you can drag buttons to change their order on a toolbar when you have the Customize Toolbars dialog box on-screen.

Creating a custom toolbar

You can use the Custom toolbar to build your own personalized toolbar, including your own choice of buttons.

▶ **To create a custom toolbar**

1. From the View menu, choose Toolbars.

   The Toolbars dialog box appears.

2. In the Toolbars dialog box, select the Custom check box and then choose OK.

   The Custom toolbar appears in the middle of the PowerPoint window.

3. Move the Custom toolbar to the side of the window so you can see it when the Customize Toolbars dialog box appears.

4. From the Tools menu, choose Customize.

   The Customize Toolbars dialog box appears.

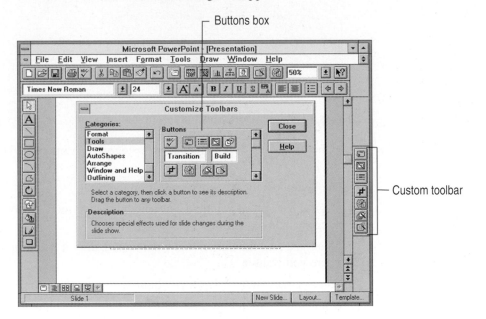

Drag buttons from the Buttons box to create a custom toolbar.

5. In the Categories box, select a tool category that includes the button you want to add.

   The buttons in the category appear on the right.

6. When you find the button you want to add, drag it to the Custom toolbar and drop the button on the toolbar.

   The button is added to the toolbar.

7. Drag as many buttons as you want to your Custom toolbar.

   You can now move the toolbar and change its shape if you want.

Understanding PowerPoint Views

As you create a presentation, you can switch among five views of your
presentation. Each view gives you a different way of looking at your work and
offers different capabilities. To switch between views, click the button that
represents the view you want. The View buttons are at the bottom left of the
PowerPoint window.

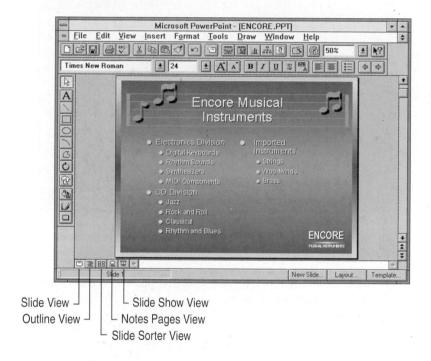

Slide View ⌐
Outline View ⌐   ⌐ Slide Show View
                      ⌐ Notes Pages View
        ⌐ Slide Sorter View

Slide View

Slide View button

You start with three toolbars in Slide view.

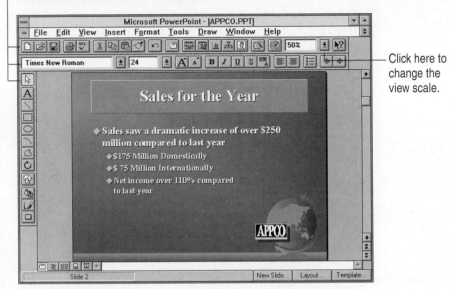

Click here to change the view scale.

In Slide view, you can type, draw, add clip art, insert pictures, and change the look of your text and objects.

In Slide view, you work on one slide at a time. You can type text, change the slide layout, add graphics, draw shapes, and add artwork and graphics from other applications.

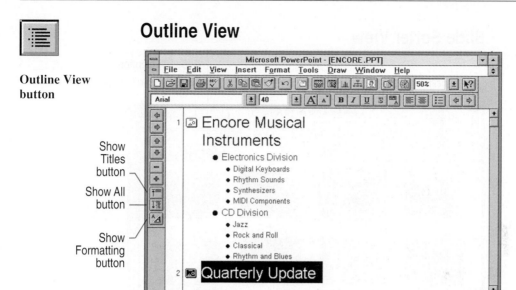

Outline View
button

Outline View

Show
Titles
button

Show All
button

Show
Formatting
button

You can display formatted or plain text and show titles only or full text in Outline view.

In Outline view, you work only with slide titles and main text in the classic outline form. It's a great way to organize your presentation and quickly develop your content.

Slide Sorter View button

Slide Sorter View

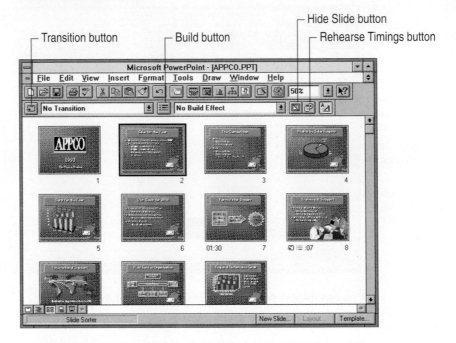

You can set slide transitions, hide slides, and create build slides in Slide Sorter view.

In Slide Sorter view, you see a miniature of each slide, complete with graphics and text. Working in Slide Sorter view is like working with slides on a light table or spreading out the pages of a report so you can see them all at once. You're able to see how your presentation flows. In Slide Sorter view, you can reorder slides, add transitions, and set timing for electronic presentations.

**Notes Pages View
button**

Notes Pages View

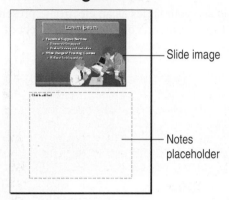

— Slide image

— Notes
placeholder

In Notes Pages view, you can type notes to use as a guide during your presentation.

In Notes Pages view, you create speaker's notes for any or all of the slides in your presentation. Each notes page corresponds to a slide. You can draw or type while in Notes Pages view just as you do in Slide view.

Slide Show View

Slide Show View button

In Slide Show view, you see your slides as an electronic presentation on your computer. Each slide fills the screen. You can see the effect of the transitions and timing that you set in Slide Sorter view.

Slide Show view fills the screen with your electronic presentation. Try using transitions and build slides for special effects.

Working with PowerPoint Commands

A command is an instruction that tells PowerPoint to do something. PowerPoint provides several ways for you to choose commands. You can choose commands from a menu or toolbar, or you can use shortcut menus or shortcut keys.

Toolbar Commands

PowerPoint toolbars provide you with one-step access to lots of tasks. You can change your view, shadow an object, print your presentation, add a graph, change a color, and much more—all with just the click of a button on one of the PowerPoint toolbars.

When you start PowerPoint, you'll notice that the slide area is surrounded by several toolbars that contain shortcut buttons for everything from Cut and Paste, to Print, to Shadow.

When you click on some buttons, PowerPoint applies the default settings for the tool you are using. For example, when you first open PowerPoint, you start with a preset default fill color. To change the fill color for an object, just choose another color, using the Colors And Lines command on the Format menu.

Some buttons, such as the ones that format text (the Italic and the Bold buttons, for example) and the ones that change the look of an object (Apply Shadow, for example), are on/off switches, or toggles. You click the button once to turn it on and click it again to turn it off.

For more information about each of the PowerPoint toolbars, see Appendix D, "PowerPoint Toolbars and Tools."

Menu Commands

Commands are grouped in menus. Some commands carry out an action immediately; others display a dialog box so that you can select options. You'll know that a command will display a dialog box if it is followed by an ellipsis.

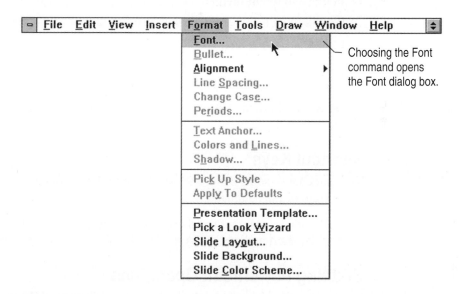

Choosing the Font command opens the Font dialog box.

Shortcut Menus

Shortcut menus give you quick access to common commands you use with objects. Shortcut menus are particularly useful because they show only commands and actions that are relevant to the selected object. If no object is selected, a menu with editing and view options will appear.

Here's an example of an object and a shortcut menu showing the commands that you can use with that object.

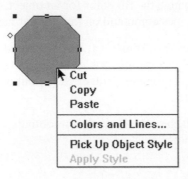

Press the right mouse button (Windows) or CTRL+click (Macintosh) to use a shortcut menu.

▶ **To display shortcut menus**

1. Point to the object for which you want to use a shortcut menu.

2. Click the *right* mouse button (Windows).

   −or−

   Press the CTRL key and click the mouse button (Macintosh).

   When the shortcut menu appears, you can choose the command you want.

   To cancel the shortcut menu, click outside the menu or press ESC.

Shortcut Keys

You can choose some commands by pressing the shortcut keys listed on the menu to the right of the command.

PowerPoint uses many of the shortcut keys found in other Microsoft products. For a list of the shortcut keys, see Appendix C, "PowerPoint Keyboard Shortcuts."

Undo button

Undoing PowerPoint Operations

Everyone makes mistakes—that's the nature of creation. When you find you've inadvertently deleted a slide, or if you don't like a change you've made to text or a picture, just choose the Undo command from the Edit menu, or click the Undo button on the Standard toolbar. This undoes your last action.

When you're about to make radical changes to an existing presentation, it's a good idea to save a copy of the presentation under a different name. That way, if you don't like the new version, you'll still have a copy of the original. To do this, just choose the Save As command from the File menu; then feel free to experiment.

PowerPoint Wizards

Wizards are PowerPoint's way of making it easy for you to quickly and efficiently create professional-looking presentations. Even if you know very little about PowerPoint, the wizards can help you develop your ideas and design your presentation.

A wizard is a guided approach to creating a presentation. All you do is answer the questions that appear on-screen.

**AutoContent
Wizard button**

The AutoContent Wizard

The AutoContent wizard helps you communicate your ideas in a clear, progressive style that lends itself to a presentation format.

This wizard starts with a title slide and then helps you choose from a selection of presentation categories— subjects such as Selling a Product, Service, or an Idea; Recommending a Strategy; or Communicating Bad News.

Once you have a title and subject, PowerPoint makes an outline for you to follow, based on how you answered the wizard's prompts. Then just type your information over the placeholder text. You can switch to Slide view to see your slides and change the slide layout.

▶ **To start the AutoContent wizard**

1. From the File menu, choose New, and then, in the New Presentation dialog box, select AutoContent Wizard.

2. Follow the instructions that appear on the screen.

**Pick A Look
Wizard button**

The Pick a Look Wizard

The Pick a Look wizard helps you create the look or the "style" of your presentation. You'll pick a template from the collection of PowerPoint designs and then tell the wizard what kind of finishing touches you want, such as automatic page numbers. The wizard customizes the Slide Master, based on your responses.

You can use the Pick a Look wizard any time you want, not just for a new presentation. That means you can organize the contents of your presentation and then let the Pick a Look wizard help you design its appearance.

▶ **To start the Pick a Look wizard**

1. On the Standard toolbar, click the Pick A Look Wizard button.

2. Follow the instructions that appear on the screen.

Quick Steps for Creating a Presentation

If you're new to presentation graphics, you can jump right into PowerPoint and make a quick presentation.

1

Start PowerPoint

Once you've installed PowerPoint, it's a simple matter to get up and running. All you need to do is double-click the PowerPoint icon in the Program Manager (Windows) or on the Desktop (Macintosh).

2

Use the AutoContent Wizard to Create a Presentation

When PowerPoint opens, you see the PowerPoint startup dialog box. Select the AutoContent Wizard option button.

You can start a new presentation with a wizard or a template or use the format of the default presentation.

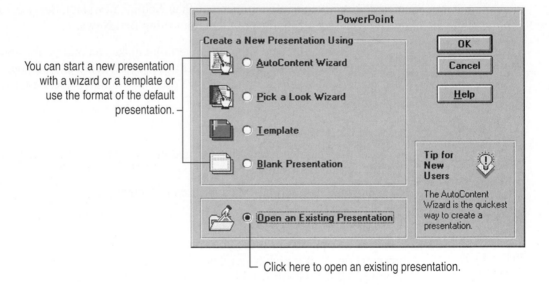

Click here to open an existing presentation.

The AutoContent wizard prompts you to make a title slide and then leads you through choosing a presentation category. You will get an outline that reflects the category you have chosen. Type your own ideas over the sample text in the outline. Switch to Slide view to see your slides.

3

Refine Your Presentation

Once you finish the first draft of a presentation, you'll probably want to go back and touch it up. That might include editing the text, changing colors, changing the order of the slides, or changing the look.

To change your presentation's look, you can apply a template or use the Pick a Look wizard.

Edit Your Text in Outline View

Use Outline view to move the text around on your slides or to edit it.

You can create or edit a presentation by typing directly in Outline view. If you have art on your slides, you'll see a graphic on the slide icon.

Edit Color and Artwork

You have lots of options:

- Change the template (there are more than 100) of your presentation by clicking the Pick A Look Wizard button on the Standard toolbar and following the on-screen instructions.

- Customize your presentation by adding clip art and by drawing shapes on the slides with the PowerPoint drawing tools. Use the Drawing toolbars to draw shapes, and then add color and patterns to the shapes. You can insert clip art by using the Insert Clip Art button. Or, you can use art from other applications, using the Picture command on the Insert menu.

Add Special Effects to Your Electronic Presentation

You can have the bullet points on the slides appear one at a time, using special effects (called creating build slides). And you can use special transitions to move to each slide in a slide show (called adding transitions). To create a build slide, go to Slide Sorter view, choose the Build command from the Tools menu, and then select the special effects you want. To add transitions, choose the Transition command from the Tools menu, and then select a transition.

Preview Your Presentation On-Screen

Preview your show by clicking the Slide Show button at the bottom of the PowerPoint window.

Slide Show button

Click the mouse button to advance the slides manually.

5 Save and Print Your Presentation

Before printing your presentation, it's a good idea to save it using the Save command on the File menu.

When you use the Pick a Look wizard, PowerPoint sets the output format for you. All you need to do is choose the Print command from the File menu. In the Print dialog box, choose what you want to print—choose Slides, for instance, to print a hard copy of your slides.

When you finish working on your presentation and are ready to quit PowerPoint, from the File menu, choose the Exit command (Windows) or the Quit command (Macintosh).

CHAPTER 2

Creating Presentations and Slides

The heart of your work in PowerPoint involves creating presentations. To create presentations, you write and design slides. Here you'll find out about making new presentations and saving the work you do. You'll learn about AutoLayouts and the placeholders that make it easy to add text, objects, and graphics. For overall presentation design, you'll find out how to use the professionally designed PowerPoint templates. You can apply one to a presentation at any time—when you begin, as you work, or after you've typed your content. The PowerPoint Slide Master—the slide that holds the format for your titles, text, and any background items you want to appear on your slides—is explained, along with how to choose and work with color schemes.

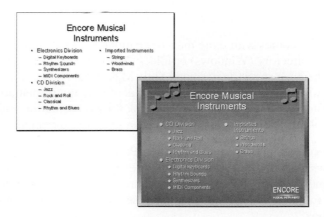

Pick a slide layout, and type your content. Then apply a look to your presentation.

In This Chapter

About Creating Presentations and Slides

In PowerPoint, your entire presentation is in one file—everything is "under one roof." That includes all the slides, the outline, the speaker's notes, and the handouts, as well as the formatting information you build into your presentation.

Using a slide layout is an easy way to begin building a presentation. You choose a slide layout by selecting New Slide from the Insert menu and then selecting the layout you want in the New Slide dialog box. There is a variety of slide layouts, some with placeholders in which you type text, and some with placeholders set up to make it easy to add graphs, charts, clip art, or other objects.

With PowerPoint, you can change the look of your presentation—the format of it, the colors in it, or the kind of output you want—anytime. You can always apply a new template or change the color scheme.

PowerPoint comes with more than 100 templates—they're in the PowerPoint Template directory (Windows) or folder (Macintosh). Each template has its own color scheme, a specially designed Slide Master, and styled fonts that work with the overall design of the presentation. In addition, any presentation can be used as a template. So, if you create a special look for a presentation and want to use the same look for other presentations, you can save it as a template.

In addition to saving a presentation as a PowerPoint file, you can save it as Windows metafiles or as a Scrapbook file on the Macintosh. Or you can save it as an outline. You also have the option of saving your presentation in PowerPoint 3.0 file format. Your choices appear in the Save File As Type box in the Save As dialog box.

Note You can open presentations created by other presentation packages directly in PowerPoint if you've installed the appropriate program translator. The PowerPoint Setup program gives you the option of installing translators for some popular applications.

This is the layout
for a title slide.

When you click a
layout, its name
appears here.

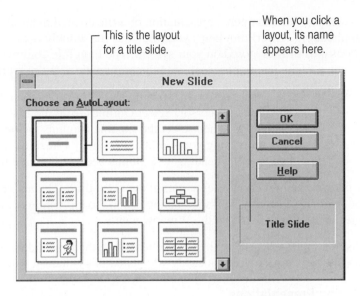

There are 21 slide layouts. Scroll to see the rest of them.

Opening and Saving Presentations

You'll find that opening and saving your presentations are pretty much the same
as in other Microsoft applications. PowerPoint helps you get started with new
presentations by creating a look and setting up the organization with wizards.

Opening Presentations

When you open a new presentation, you can choose from among a variety of
formats and ways of working. For example, you can start with the AutoContent
wizard to help you organize what you want your presentation to say. You can use
the Pick a Look wizard to help you open a template and set up your masters. Or
you can choose to start with a blank presentation, which gives you the PowerPoint
default format. In other words, you don't have to start from scratch for each new
presentation.

Quite often, you'll want to create a new presentation using the format of a
presentation you've already made. For example, if your business uses a standard
format for presentations, you can open a new presentation that uses that standard
format. When you choose New from the File menu, you'll be given an
opportunity to use the format of the current presentation.

Both Windows and Macintosh PowerPoint 4.0 files can be opened on either
platform. You can open files from all versions of PowerPoint (such as 2.0 or 3.0
presentations) on the platform you're using—that is, Windows users can open
older Windows files, and Macintosh users can open older Macintosh files.

When you want to open a presentation or a file created in another Microsoft application, PowerPoint helps you find your file quickly—even if you have thousands of files stored on your system. The Find File command can help you locate a file to open or to insert into the presentation you're working on.

You can create a presentation by opening an outline you created using Microsoft Word or another word processor. Select Outlines from the List Files Of Type box in the Open dialog box. Then select the file that contains the outline. PowerPoint creates a presentation using your outline. Each major heading in the outline becomes a slide, and the heading's subpoints become bulleted lists on the slide.

You can open several presentations at the same time. The active presentation, the one you are currently working on, appears in the top window. All open presentations are listed on the Window menu.

As you highlight a file in the Open dialog box, the first slide in the file appears in the preview box so you can easily verify that this is the file you want.

Saving Presentations

When you close a file, PowerPoint checks to see whether you've made changes to it. If you haven't made any changes, the file closes. If you have made changes, PowerPoint asks you whether you want to save them.

If you've opened more than one presentation, only the active one is saved when you choose Save or Save As. To save another open presentation, click it to make it active, and then save it.

You can save your slides as pictures—as a metafile (Windows) or as a Scrapbook file (Macintosh)—which you can then insert in other applications. You can also save an outline as a rich text format (RTF) file, and then open and edit it in another application. Choose Save As from the File menu. Then select the type of file you want in the Save File As Type box. Select Outline for an RTF file; select Windows Metafile (Windows) or Scrapbook (Macintosh) for a picture.

If you're planning to distribute a presentation and you want to ensure that the fonts you use will be displayed or printed, you can embed the fonts in the presentation.

You can save a presentation as a PowerPoint 3.0 file for use with PowerPoint 3.0, or with the PowerPoint Viewer that came with PowerPoint 3.0, so that you can share the presentations you create in PowerPoint 4.0 with others who are using PowerPoint 3.0. When you save a 4.0 presentation as a 3.0 file, dashed lines become solid and any rotated text or objects won't be rotated. Also, hidden slides will appear as normal slides in your presentation. If you've linked or embedded objects, they'll be available to you if both the application and the source document are available. Otherwise, they'll appear as pictures.

For in-depth procedures, in online Help see:

- Creating your own default presentation
- Saving slides as pictures to use in other applications
- Saving a presentation with embedded fonts
- PowerPoint 4.0 features not supported when saving as a PowerPoint 3.0 file

under "How to Open and Save Presentations—In Depth" in the Chapter 2 Help Contents window.

Tip You can avoid accidentally overwriting a file by giving files unique names when you save them. If you try to save a file with a name that already exists, an alert warns you and gives you a chance to cancel what you're doing and rename the file you're saving. You can't recover a file that's been replaced with another one.

Terms That Apply to Presentations

Template A presentation whose format and color scheme you apply to another presentation. More than 100 professionally designed templates come with PowerPoint, but you can use any presentation as a template anytime.

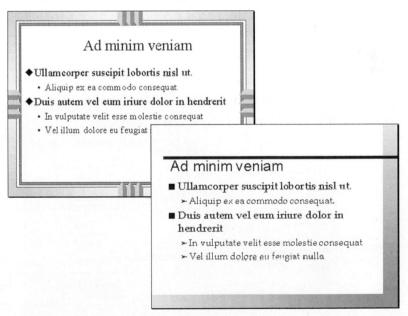

You can change the look of a presentation at any time. Just apply a different template.

PowerPoint default presentation PowerPoint comes with a default presentation, complete with color scheme, type styles, and so on. This is the presentation format you are working with when you choose Blank Presentation in the New Presentation dialog box. You can make any presentation the default by saving it as DEFAULT.PPT (Windows) or Default Presentation (Macintosh). Your presentation will overwrite the PowerPoint default presentation and will be stored in the PowerPoint directory (Windows) or folder (Macintosh). Then, each time you open a blank presentation, the defaults will be the ones you set.

Masters In PowerPoint, you have a master for each of the key components in your presentation—one for slides, one for your outline, one for speaker's notes, and one for audience handouts. Pictures and text you include on the masters will appear on every slide and notes page. The Slide Master and Notes Master are particularly flexible. You can move objects around (including the title and text placeholders), add art, add headings or labels, change colors, change fonts, and so on.

How to Open and Save Presentations

Creating a new presentation

When you create a new presentation, you have choices about how to proceed. You can use the AutoContent wizard to help you organize what you want your presentation to say. You can use the Pick a Look wizard to help you apply a template and set up the masters. You can also start with a "blank" presentation if you want to use the default presentation—either the PowerPoint default or one that you set up.

▶ **To create a new presentation**

1. Double-click the PowerPoint icon to open the application.

   The PowerPoint startup dialog box appears.

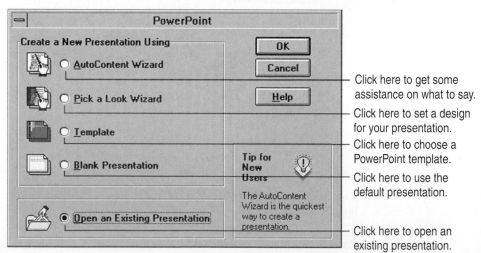

Click here to get some assistance on what to say.

Click here to set a design for your presentation.

Click here to choose a PowerPoint template.

Click here to use the default presentation.

Click here to open an existing presentation.

2. Choose the way you want to create your new presentation.

To begin by following along with a wizard, select the button of the wizard you want, and then choose OK. The wizard you selected appears on the screen. Follow the instructions and enter the information requested.

To start with a template and establish a particular look for your presentation, select the Template button, and then choose OK. The Presentation Template dialog box appears. Choose the template you want, and then choose Apply.

To begin with the blank default presentation, select the Blank Presentation button. Then choose OK.

Opening an existing presentation

You can open several presentations at once while you're working in PowerPoint. When you open an existing presentation, the view and scale are the same as when you last saved it.

▶ **To open an existing presentation**

- From the File menu, choose the file you want to open from the list of recently used files.

–or–

1. From the File menu, choose Open.

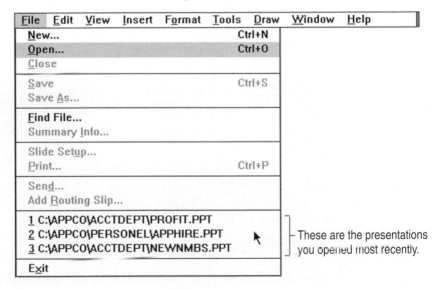

These are the presentations you opened most recently.

2. Select the presentation you want to open, and choose OK.

Switch directories, folders, or disk drives as needed to find the presentation you want.

Tip You can open a file other than a presentation, even if you're not sure of its file type, by choosing Open from the File menu and then selecting All Files in the List Files Of Type box. You'll see all the files in that directory (Windows) or folder (Macintosh).

Finding a file or presentation

A Find File button is available when you're opening a file, inserting slides as a presentation or as an outline, or inserting pictures. Choose it to open a dialog box that lets you identify the directory and the file you want to find. If the files were created using an application that doesn't support Summary Information, PowerPoint will not be able to find a match using only the Advanced Search Summary information. It will find your file, however, when you provide the filename, location, and/or the time stamp information.

▶ **To find a file or presentation**

1. From the File menu, choose Open.

   The Open dialog box appears.

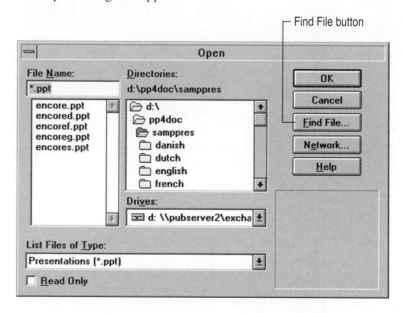

You can use all the Find File features to locate a presentation if you fill in the Summary Info dialog box for that presentation.

2. In the File Name box, type the name of the file you are looking for.
3. Choose Find File.

Saving and naming a presentation

You use the Save As command to name a presentation when you save it for the first time. You can also use this command to save an existing presentation with a new name.

▶ **To save a presentation for the first time**

1. From the File menu, choose Save As.

   The Save As dialog box appears.

2. Type the name of the presentation.

   Because this is the first time you're saving the presentation, you need to give it a name in the File Name box (Windows) or the Save Presentation As box (Macintosh).

   You can save your presentation on another disk drive and in any directory (Windows) or folder (Macintosh) that you want.

3. When you've typed the presentation name and placed it in the directory or folder you want, choose OK.

▶ **To save an existing presentation with a new name**

1. From the File menu, choose Save As.

2. Type the new name you want to use for the presentation in the Save As box.

   You can save the presentation on any disk drive and in any directory (Windows) or folder (Macintosh) you want.

3. When you've typed the new name and located the directory or folder you want, choose OK.

   Your presentation stays on the screen—with the new name in the title bar.

Tip Before editing an existing presentation that you have opened, choose Save As on the File menu, and then give the presentation another name. Then work on the newly created duplicate version. This way, when you make changes to the presentation, the original presentation will not be affected.

Closing presentations

▶ **To close a presentation**

1. From the File menu, choose Close.

   −or−

   Double-click the presentation's Close box (Windows) or single-click the presentation's Close box (Macintosh).

   −or−

   Press CTRL+F4 (Windows).

If you've made changes to the presentation since you last saved it, PowerPoint asks whether you want to save your changes before closing.

2. Choose Yes (Windows) or Save (Macintosh) to save your changes and close the presentation.

If you *don't* want to save your changes, choose No (Windows) or Don't Save (Macintosh) and PowerPoint will close the file without saving your changes.

If you change your mind about closing the file, choose Cancel.

Entering summary information

You can enter information in the Summary Info dialog box that records the title, the subject, and other key information that helps you keep track of your presentations.

▶ **To enter summary information**

1. From the File menu, choose Summary Info.

   The Summary Info dialog box appears.

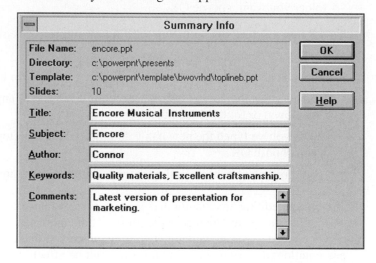

Fill in the Summary Info dialog box so you can use the Find File features to locate your presentations later.

2. Enter information in the dialog box as appropriate:

   - In the Title box, type a name for the presentation. This title can be longer and more descriptive than the presentation's file name.

   - In the Subject box, type a brief description of the presentation's contents.

   - In the Author box, type the name of the presentation's author. By default, this is the name you typed when installing PowerPoint.

- In the Keywords box, type words that you associate with the presentation so you can find it using Find File. You can copy and paste the titles of your slides into the Keywords box, if you want.

- In the Comments box, type any comments you feel are appropriate.

3. Choose OK.

Tip You can turn off the Summary Info dialog box if you don't want it to appear when you first save a document. From the Tools menu, choose Options, and then clear the Prompt For Summary Info check box.

Working with Slides and Layouts

When you create a new presentation in PowerPoint, you begin with one slide. As you build the presentation, you'll be adding more slides—some with text, some with artwork, and some with charts.

You can add a slide or slides to your presentation anytime you want by choosing New Slide from the Insert menu or by clicking the New Slide button on the status bar. It doesn't matter which of the PowerPoint views you're in—PowerPoint adds the slide following your current, or active, slide. However, if you are working in one of the masters, the new slide becomes the first slide in your presentation. You choose the layout of a new slide by picking the AutoLayout you want to use in the New Slide dialog box.

You'll see placeholders for various objects on the AutoLayouts—some for titles and text, and some for clip art, graphs, or organizational charts. The placeholders give you quick access to many PowerPoint visuals. You just double-click inside a placeholder to immediately add the kind of object specified in the placeholder. Or single-click to add text to any placeholder.

For in-depth procedures, in online Help see:

- Changing the kind of placeholder on a slide

under "How to Work with Slides and Layouts—In Depth" in the Chapter 2 Help Contents window.

Terms That Apply to Slides and Layouts

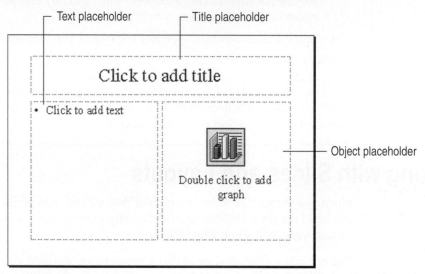

Text placeholder   Title placeholder

Click to add title

• Click to add text

Double click to add graph

Object placeholder

Here's a slide layout that's set up for your title, a bulleted list, and a graph. To change layouts, click the Layout button on the status bar.

AutoLayout   The slide layouts that are available when you add a new slide to a presentation. AutoLayouts contain ready-made placeholders for titles, text, and objects such as clip art, graphs, and charts. You can change layouts whenever you want using the Layout button on the status bar.

Title placeholder   The title box that appears when you create a new slide. Click in the title placeholder and type your slide title.

AutoLayout object area   The box or boxes, in addition to the title placeholder, that appear when you create a new slide. There are many kinds of object placeholders: placeholders for text, graphs, tables, organizational charts, and clip art. Just click to add text in a placeholder, or double-click to add the specified object.

How to Work with Slides and Layouts

Creating a new slide

PowerPoint offers you a variety of AutoLayouts every time you create a new slide.

▶ **To create a new slide**

1. From the Insert menu, choose New Slide.

   −or−

   Click the New Slide button on the status bar.

   −or−

   Press CTRL+M (Windows) or COMMAND+M (Macintosh).

   The New Slide dialog box appears.

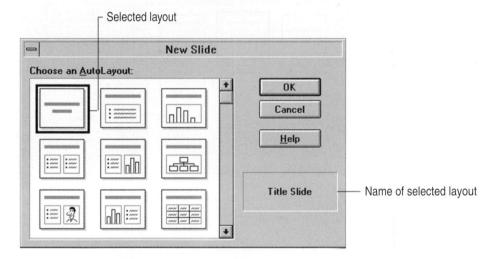

Using slide layouts lets you start with a format that matches what you want to create.

   Use the scroll bar to see more layouts.

2. Select the layout you want, and then choose OK.

   The new slide with placeholders for title and/or text and/or objects appears on your screen. Notice how the placeholders correspond to the layout you selected.

Changing a layout for a slide

As you create a presentation or as you edit an existing presentation, you may want to change the layout of a slide. You don't lose any text or graphics when a slide adopts a new layout. You can resize the text or graphics boxes to conform to the new layout.

▶ **To change a slide's layout**

1. While in Slide view, from the Format menu, choose Slide Layout.

   –or–

   Click the Layout button on the status bar.

   The Slide Layout dialog box appears with the current layout highlighted.

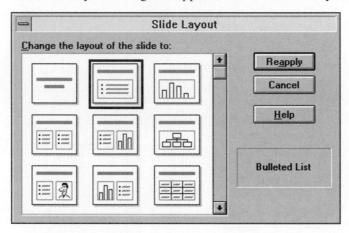

You can change the layout of any slide at any time using the Layout button on the status bar.

2. Click the new slide layout you want, and then choose Apply.

Bulleted List layout ⌐   Text & Clip Art layout ⌐

   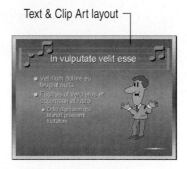

You can change layouts after you create a slide. Here, you can add clip art next to your bulleted list.

Deleting a slide

You can delete one or more slides from your presentation in several ways. If you only have one slide in your presentation, it can only be deleted in Slide Sorter or Outline view.

▶ **To delete a slide**

- In Slide or Notes view, from the Edit menu, choose Delete Slide.

  −or−

  In Slide Sorter or Outline view, select the slide or slides you want to delete, and then, from the Edit menu, choose Delete Slide, or press the BACKSPACE or DELETE key (Windows) or the DELETE key (Macintosh).

Changing the order of your slides

When you're in Outline view or Slide Sorter view, it's easy to change the order in which your slides appear in your presentation.

▶ **To change the order of your slides in Outline view**

- To move a slide from one location to another in Outline view, select the slide, and then drag the title icon from its present spot to its new spot.

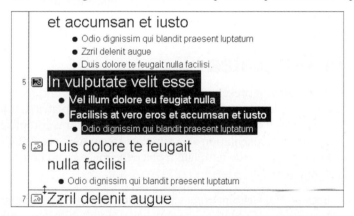

As you drag the slide icon, a horizontal line appears to make placement easier.

While you're dragging the icon, a horizontal line appears to make it easier for you to place the slide just where you want it.

▶ **To change the order of your slides in Slide Sorter view**

- To move a slide in Slide Sorter view, drag the selected slide from its present location to its new location.

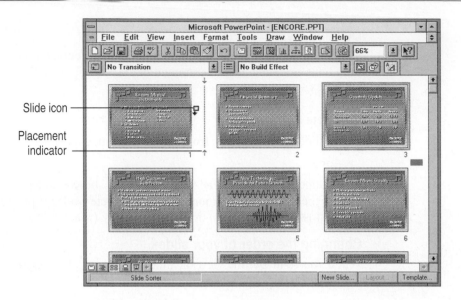

Slide icon

Placement indicator

As you drag a slide in Slide Sorter view, a slide icon appears above the pointer.

As you drag the slide, a slide icon appears above the pointer. When you reach a spot between two slides where you can place the slide, an indicator shows you where the slide will appear in the presentation.

Working with Templates

A template is a presentation in which the masters and the colors have been especially designed for a particular "look." Templates define what your text will look like and where it will appear, and they offer a complete color scheme. When you apply a presentation as a template to an open presentation, the master and color scheme of the template replace the master and color scheme of the open presentation.

Although PowerPoint comes with more than 100 artist-created templates, any PowerPoint presentation can serve as a template for any other presentation at any time. The best way to understand what templates can do for a presentation is to browse through the templates in the Appendix, where you'll find printed versions of some of the templates that come with PowerPoint.

You may prefer to start by applying a template to a new presentation. Or you may want to apply a template after you've created part or all of a presentation. In any case, just follow the procedure called "To apply a template" in the following section. It works the same way whether you're starting a new presentation or working on an existing one. If you find that you don't like the look of a template you've just applied, simply apply a different one.

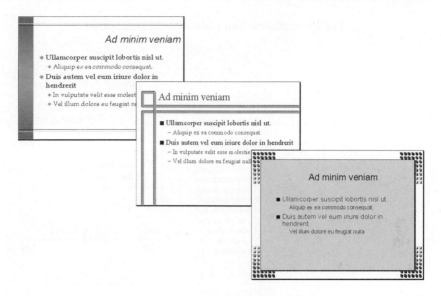

You can use the PowerPoint templates or one you create yourself.

How to Work with Templates

Applying a template

You can apply a template to a new or an existing presentation. A template applies to all the slides in your presentation. The act of applying a template cannot be undone.

▶ **To apply a template**

1. From the Format menu, choose Presentation Template.

   –or–

   Click the Template button on the status bar.

Template button

The Presentation Template dialog box appears.

Preview box

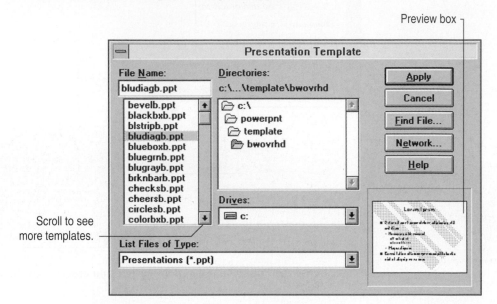

Scroll to see
more templates.

Templates are stored according to what you are producing: color slides, black-and-white overheads, or color overheads.

2. Click a template name to preview the template in the Preview box.

    When you select the name of a template file, a slide appears in the Preview box so you can see the template's color scheme and get an idea of the design.

3. Double-click a template name to open the file and apply it to all the slides in your presentation.

Tip   You can apply a new template to a presentation even if you've already applied another template. The new one merely replaces the old one. The act of applying a template cannot be undone. If you think you might want to use the old template again, be sure to save at least one slide that uses it as a presentation.

Working with the Slide Master

The Slide Master is the slide that holds the format for the title and text. Here's where you add the background items that you want to appear on every slide in a presentation. A Slide Master directs the styles of the titles and text in your presentation. If you make a change to the Slide Master (choosing a special font for the text, for example, or italicizing the slide title), the change affects all slides in your presentation that follow the master.

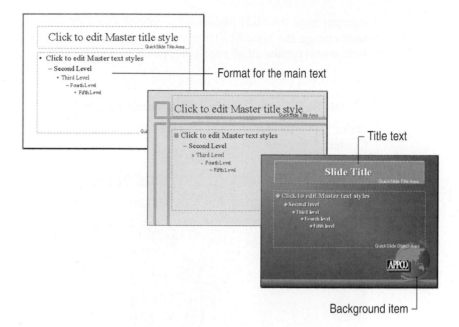

Format for the main text

Title text

Background item

The Slide Master is the slide that holds the format for the title and the text, as well as the background items that you want to appear on every slide.

Some things on a Slide Master are set up by PowerPoint (such as a place for slide titles and text) so you don't have to create them each time. Others you can add to a master (such as your logo or the page number stamp). If you have objects that you want to appear on each slide in your presentation, put them on the Slide Master. You only have to create common items once. PowerPoint automatically includes them on every slide.

You can change the Slide Master's format anytime—before, during, or after you create a presentation. For instance, you may decide at the last minute that you want to add your company name to every slide. Just use the Text tool to type it outside the placeholders on the Slide Master, and PowerPoint will apply it to all the slides in the presentation in a single step.

Not every slide has to follow the Slide Master. Slides use the color scheme of the Slide Master, but individual slides can have their own color schemes. This way you can use different color schemes for different sections in your presentation.

As you create a slide, you have the option of using or not using the elements from the Slide Master. You can use the master title, the master text, the background items, and the color scheme as you please on each slide.

To change the entire presentation, change the format of the Slide Master. PowerPoint then changes all of your slides accordingly. Any changes you make to the format of the title and text on individual slides are retained by PowerPoint as exceptions to the Slide Master—exceptions that only you can change. So if you later change the Slide Master or apply a template, PowerPoint applies the new format and retains all of your exceptions.

For in-depth procedures, in online Help see:

▪ Adding the time and date and numbering slides

under "How to Work with the Slide Master—In Depth" in the Chapter 2 Help Contents window.

Terms That Apply to the Slide Master

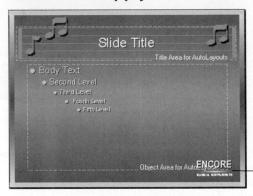

Use your logo as a background item.

Slide Master   The slide that holds the formatted placeholders for the title and text as well as any background items that you want to appear on your slides. If you make a change to the Slide Master, the change affects all slides in your presentation that follow the master.

Master title (Title Area for AutoLayouts)   The formatted placeholder for slide titles on the Slide Master. Here's where you set the font, color, size, and alignment of slide titles as well as the title's attributes (fill, line, and shadow), shape, and placement on the slide.

Master text (Object Area for AutoLayouts)   The formatted placeholder for the main slide text on the Slide Master. Here's where you set the font, color, size, line spacing, and alignment of the main text as well as the text's attributes (fill, line, and shadow), shape, and placement on the slide.

Title format   The object and text attributes of the master title.

Text format   The object and text attributes of the master text.

Background items   Those objects you add to the Slide Master so that they'll appear on all of the slides in a presentation that follow the master. PowerPoint considers any object on the master—other than the master title and master text—

to be a background item. Background items typically include art (such as a logo), the date, the time, the page or slide number, and the name of the presentation.

Note Text that you type into the text placeholders on the Slide Master won't show up on your slides—the placeholders are for formatting the text style. If you want text to appear on the slides, create a new text box on the Slide Master, using the Text tool on the Drawing toolbar. Then type your text.

How to Work with the Slide Master

Changing a Slide Master

When you change any of the attributes on the Slide Master, the change is reflected on all of the slides in your presentation that follow the master.

▶ **To change a Slide Master**

1. From the View menu, choose Master, and then choose Slide Master.

   The Slide Master appears. You can work on the master just as you would a slide—adding a logo, changing text attributes, and so forth.

2. When you finish making changes, from the View menu, choose Slides.

   Now, when you look at the slides in your presentation, you see the changes you made applied to every slide.

Making a slide that differs from the Slide Master

You can change the look of any of the slides in your presentation without changing the Slide Master. You can vary how the slides look throughout your presentation if you want.

▶ **To make a slide that differs from the Slide Master**

- Display the slide you want to change. Then you can change the font size and color, background colors, and the color scheme.

  Changes you make won't affect other slides or the Slide Master.

Note You can change a slide so its attributes differ from the Slide Master, but you can't apply a template to an individual slide. Whenever you apply a template, the entire presentation is affected, and any background items you have added and any changes you have made to the master title or master text will be lost.

Reapplying the Slide Master title and text format to a slide

If you've changed the master title or text on a slide and you decide you want the slide to follow the master, you can reapply the Slide Master.

▶ **To reapply the master title and text format to a slide**

1. Display the slide to which you want to reapply the Slide Master.
2. From the Format menu, choose Slide Layout.

   The Slide Layout dialog box appears with the current slide's layout selected.
3. Choose Reapply.

   The text and placeholders on the slide now conform to the Slide Master.

Note Reapplying the slide layout will not affect the slide color scheme.

Reapplying the Slide Master color scheme to a slide

If you've changed colors on a slide—whether background, text, or fill color—you can reapply the Slide Master color scheme.

▶ **To reapply the Slide Master color scheme**

1. Display the slide to which you want to reapply the Slide Master color scheme.
2. From the Format menu, choose Slide Color Scheme.

   The Slide Color Scheme dialog box appears.
3. Choose Follow Master.
4. Choose Apply.

   The colors on the slide now conform to the Slide Master.

Removing background items from a slide

You can remove background items on a slide-by-slide basis.

▶ **To remove background items from a slide**

1. Display the slide from which you want to remove background items.
2. From the Format menu, choose Slide Background.

   The Slide Background dialog box appears.
3. Clear the Display Objects On This Slide check box, and then choose Apply.

Hints for designing a Slide Master

- Consider adding a border. A border serves as a frame for your graphics and text. You can use a border on slides to emphasize the content of the slide. A border is generally a shape such as a rounded rectangle. Most borders are oriented to the center of the Slide Master.

- Experiment with border designs. For example, you might want to try the octagon and the cross shapes for your presentation borders. Try changing the line style to make the border more stylish. Or experiment with the adjustment handle a decorative effect in the corners of the border.

- When you add background items to the Slide Master, the title and text always appear on top of the background items on your slides.

- If you delete the title or text placeholder on the Slide Master, you can restore it while you have the Slide Master on your screen by choosing the Master Layout command from the Format menu.

- You insert the date, time, or page number symbols on the masters. PowerPoint takes care of printing/displaying the correct information on each slide or page.

Creating and Changing Color Schemes

Color schemes are sets of eight balanced colors designed to be used as the main colors of a slide presentation—the text color, the background color, fill colors, and so on. Using a color scheme ensures that you'll create professional-looking slides and makes it easy for you to change colors on the slides in your presentation.

When you open a blank presentation in PowerPoint, you'll find it already has a built-in, default color scheme. As you work with PowerPoint, though, you'll probably find that you want to create your own "look." The Slide Color Scheme command on the Format menu takes you to the Slide Color Scheme dialog box, where you start choosing a color scheme for your presentation. It's also where you add other colors to the menus, rearrange colors, and change the background color. Each of these procedures is covered in this section.

The colors from which you make your choices for a scheme have been selected by professional designers. When you choose one color, the colors made available to you for your next choice are ones that have been selected by designers to complement your first choice.

A color scheme is your main palette—you use it constantly as you create your presentation. PowerPoint keeps close track of color schemes. That way, if you change your color scheme, PowerPoint can update your slides for you automatically. Other colors are not part of your color scheme, so PowerPoint doesn't keep track of them.

For in-depth procedures, in online Help see:

- Creating more colors
- Adding colors to drop-down boxes

under "How to Create and Change Color Schemes—In Depth" in the Chapter 2 Help Contents window.

Here are some ideas that will help you understand more about color schemes.

Every color menu lists the color-scheme colors as your options.   For instance, when you look at the drop-down boxes for Fill or Text Color, the eight colors offered as choices are the color-scheme colors.

You can change all the color-scheme colors in a presentation in one step.
Changing a color scheme and then applying the modified scheme to all the slides in a presentation changes the colors automatically. You don't have to recolor each slide manually. PowerPoint does it for you. But any other colors (the non-scheme colors) you're using aren't affected. You need to change them manually.

Each slide can have its own color scheme.   You can use one color scheme for the slides from the Accounting Department and separately apply another color scheme to all the slides from the Research Department. The different colors act as clues for the audience. Typically, you would limit the number of color schemes in a presentation to no more than two or three, and in many cases a single scheme is enough.

You can add colors to the color drop-down menus.   You can further customize your color choices by adding colors you like to such drop-down color menus as fill color, shadow color, and line color.

Each template comes with a color scheme.   If you apply a new template to a presentation, the color scheme changes to reflect that template. You can use that scheme as it is or change one or more of its colors.

Notes pages and audience handout pages can have their own color scheme.
This makes it possible to print your speaker's notes and audience handouts with colored text. Changing the color scheme for the notes or handout pages doesn't change the colors in the slide image.

You can copy color schemes from one presentation to another.   If you want to use the same color scheme (such as your corporate color scheme) in more than one presentation, you can copy it from one open presentation to another without having to re-create the scheme for each new presentation. Choose Pick Up Scheme and Apply Scheme from the Format menu while in Slide Sorter view.

Applying color schemes to embedded objects.   You can recolor pictures or other embedded objects you add to your presentations so they match your color scheme. Use the Recolor command on the Tools menu.

The colors you see depend on the video card in your computer.   How the colors you've chosen appear on the screen depends on the video card installed in your computer.

The following illustration shows how the eight colors in a color scheme can be used.

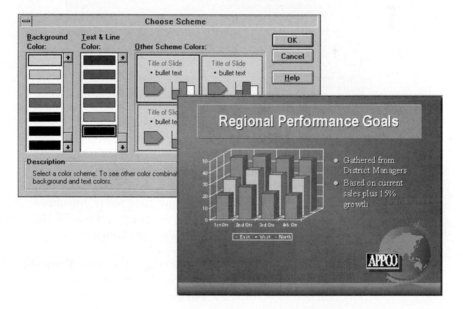

When you choose a color scheme for your presentation, PowerPoint ensures that all the colors are coordinated.

Terms That Apply to Color Schemes

Here are some basic terms you'll need to know when working with color schemes.

Color scheme   The basic set of eight colors you can assign to slides, to an individual slide, to notes pages, and to audience handouts. A color scheme consists of a background color, a color for lines and text, and six remaining colors, all balanced to provide easily readable slides. Changing a color scheme can dramatically alter the look of slides. You can change any color in your color scheme, using the Slide Color Scheme command on the Format menu.

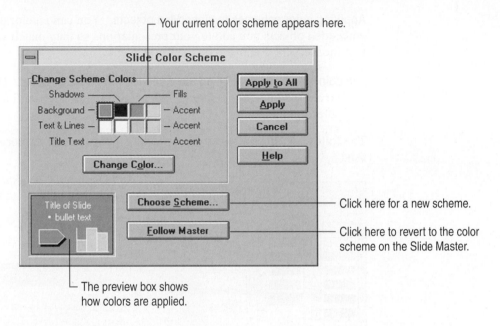

Other colors   Non-scheme colors that you use for a special purpose. You can choose or create other colors and use them along with your color scheme, for example. Non-scheme colors are not changed if you choose a different color scheme for a presentation. You'll want to use these for flags, clip art, and other objects whose colors you do not want to change.

Background color   The underlying color of a PowerPoint slide. If you're painting on a white canvas, for example, your background color is white. You can paint any other color on top of it, but the underlying color remains white; the white (the background) shows wherever you don't add paint. The background color on a slide works the same way.

Lines and text color   A color that contrasts with the background color and is used for writing text and drawing lines on the slide. The lines and text color and the background color together set the tone for a presentation. For instance, a gray background with black as the lines and text color sets a somber tone, while a light blue background with golden lines and text color sets a more upbeat, warmer tone.

Title text color   Like the lines and text color, the title text color contrasts with the background.

Shadows color   The color PowerPoint applies when you shadow an object. This color is often a darker shade of the background color.

Fills color   The fills color is one that contrasts with both the background and the lines and text colors. The fills color is used when you make graphs.

Accent colors   These colors are designed to work as colors for secondary features on a slide. Accent colors are also used as colors on graphs.

How to Create and Change Color Schemes

Choosing a new color scheme

PowerPoint comes with hundreds of color schemes, each designed to give your presentation a different look. It's easy to experiment with different color schemes.

▶   **To choose a new color scheme**

1. From the Format menu, choose Slide Color Scheme.

2. In the Slide Color Scheme dialog box, click Choose Scheme.

    The Choose Scheme dialog box appears.

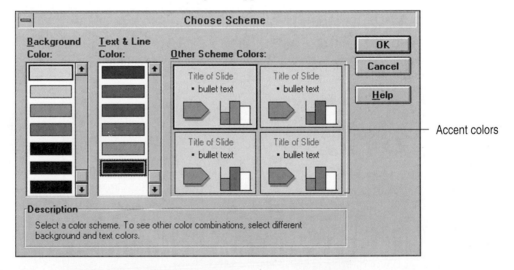

When you choose a background color, appropriate colors for text and lines appear. Accent color choices appear after you choose a color for your text.

Your new color scheme is based on the colors you select for the background and the text. You must choose a background color first, then a text color, and then a combination of other colors to complete the new color scheme.

3. Select a background color from the Background Color box.

   You can scroll the palette to see more color choices. When you select a background color, the text colors change to coordinate with the background color.

4. Choose a text and line color in the Text & Line Color box.

   You can scroll the color palette to see more color choices.

   When you choose the text and line color, four complete color schemes appear.

5. Select one of the color schemes, and choose OK.

Tip If you're working on a grayscale display, use the color identifiers on the status bar to select colors for your presentation. You can see the identifiers when you display the various Colors dialog boxes (Other Colors, Background Colors, and so on). Whenever you select a color, its abbreviation appears on the status bar.

Changing a color in a color scheme

You can change individual colors within a color scheme. For example, here's how you can change the title text of your slides to a different color.

▶ **To change a color (such as the title text) in a color scheme**

1. From the Format menu, choose Slide Color Scheme.

   The Slide Color Scheme dialog box appears.

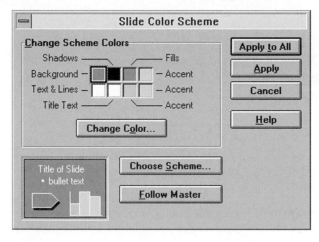

You can change one or more colors to revamp your color scheme, or you can click the Choose Scheme button to start over.

Notice how the current color scheme is represented in the bottom left of the dialog box. As you change colors, you'll get a preview of your new color scheme.

2. Select the Title Text color box, and then choose Change Color.

   The Title Text Color dialog box appears.

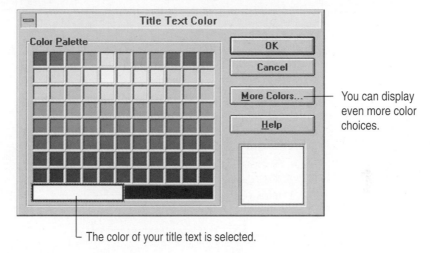

You can display even more color choices.

The color of your title text is selected.

3. Choose the color you want for your slide titles, and then choose OK.

4. If you want the color change to affect only the current slide, choose Apply.

   Or choose Apply To All to change all the slides in the presentation.

Adding a shaded background to slides

Custom backgrounds are easy to create. You can change the color and add dramatic shading to any or all of the slides in your presentation. To change the background for *all* slides, work on the Slide Master or make sure that you choose the Apply To All option.

▶ **To add a shaded background to your slides**

1. From the Format menu, choose Slide Background.

   The Slide Background dialog box appears.

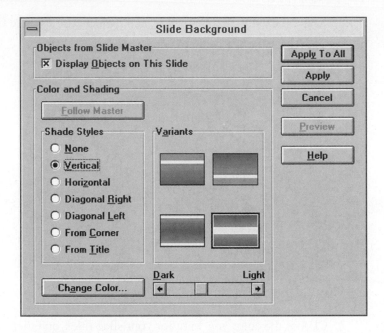

2. Select one of the options in the Shade Styles box.

   The available shading choices appear in the Variants box.

3. Click the Change Color button if you want to change the background color. Then select another color in the dialog box, and choose OK.

4. For different shading effects, slide the scroll bar on the bottom of the dialog box from dark to light. The sample slides in the Variants box change as you scroll.

5. When you're happy with your background design, choose Apply or Apply To All.

Picking up and applying a color scheme from one slide to another

If you create a color scheme that you like, you can apply it to another slide or presentation, using the Format Painter tool.

Format Painter button ▶ **To pick up and apply a color scheme**

1. In Slide Sorter view, select a slide with a color scheme that you want to apply to another slide.

2. On the Standard toolbar, click the Format Painter button.

   The color scheme is picked up.

3. Select the slide (or slides) to which you want to apply the scheme you just picked up.

   The color scheme is applied to the slide or slides.

Undoing a change to a color scheme

If you change a color scheme and decide that you don't like it, you can undo it immediately, using the Undo command.

▶ **To undo a color scheme change**

- From the Edit menu, choose Undo.

Hints for working with color schemes

- If you're not satisfied with any of the color scheme choices, try changing either the background color or the lines and text color of the scheme that most closely matches the one you want.

- Try applying your new color scheme to one slide. You can always change the slide back to the Slide Master's color scheme if you don't like what you see. From the Format menu, choose the Slide Color Scheme command. Choose Follow Master, and then choose Apply.

- If you'll be producing 35mm slides from your presentation, remember that dark backgrounds work best on slides.

- If you'll be producing overhead transparencies, use light backgrounds.

- If you have a color printer, try picking a unique color scheme for your notes pages. Color schemes you create for notes pages don't affect the color schemes of the slides in your presentation.

- Shading applies only to the background of a slide. However, you can shade a selected filled object. From the Format menu, choose the Colors And Lines command. Then choose Shaded in the Fill Color drop-down box. You can also click the Fill Color button on the Drawing+ toolbar, and then choose the Shaded option.

- You can create a dramatic 3-D effect by shading a slide's background in one direction, and then shading shapes and objects in another direction.

- If none of the colors in the Slide Color Scheme dialog box strike your fancy, select the color you want to change, click the Change Color button, and then, in the next dialog box, click the More Colors button. Use the More Colors dialog box to create a custom color.

CHAPTER 3

Working with PowerPoint Objects

All slides in a PowerPoint presentation are made up of objects. Lines, arcs, shapes, text, graphs—anything you put on a slide—are objects. What you can do with an object depends on whether you created it in PowerPoint or whether you inserted it from another application. Once you know how to manipulate the different types of objects, you've mastered a lot of what's involved in making presentations that really work.

In This Chapter

Terms That Apply to Objects

As you've already discovered, objects are the key building blocks in PowerPoint. Just about everything you work on is an object. There are different types of objects, and the behavior of an object depends on its type. PowerPoint objects are native to PowerPoint; embedded, or OLE, objects are objects you create in another application. Some of the terms used to describe working with objects may be new to you. Here are some terms you'll want to know.

Object   The text, lines, and shapes that you create using the Text and Drawing tools, and the pictures you import from other applications.

Attribute   Each aspect of an object that you can manipulate using the PowerPoint tools and commands, including line, fill, shadow, embossing, color, and shape.

Shape   Objects you create using the Text or AutoShape tools. Objects created with the Line, Arc, and Freeform tools don't have shape as an attribute.

Border   The visible line around the edge of an object. The four lines of a rectangle are its border; the three lines of a triangle are its border; and the single curved line that forms a circle is its border. You change the border's style by changing the line style for the object.

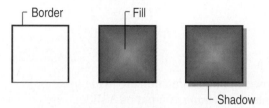

Resize handle   The square at each corner and along the sides of a selected object. Dragging a resize handle resizes the object.

Adjustment handle   A diamond that lets you adjust the dimensions of a selected object. For example, you can adjust a rounded rectangle to be more rounded or less rounded. Or, for a cross shape, you can adjust its arms to be thicker or thinner.

Control handle   A black square at a vertex of a freeform shape or a polygon. You edit freeform shapes and polygons by adding, deleting, and moving their control handles.

Picture   An image from another application. It can have some, but not all, of the attributes of an object created in PowerPoint. You can move and resize a picture and change some of its original colors. If the image is not a bitmap, you can ungroup it and break it into its component objects. These objects can then be manipulated just like any other PowerPoint object.

Selection box   The "fuzzy" outline around a text object that indicates it's selected. You can move a text object by clicking the outline and dragging.

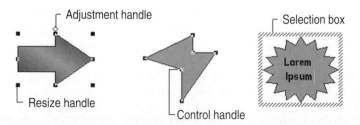

Selection rectangle The box framed by the resize handles when a graphic is selected. When you drag across an object to select it, the selection rectangle appears when you release the mouse button.

Grid An invisible network of lines that covers the slide. As you draw objects, their corners align on the nearest intersection of the grid. Although you can't see the grid, it automatically helps align objects. You can turn the grid on and off using the Snap To Grid command on the Draw menu. Or you can temporarily turn it off by holding down the ALT key (Windows) or the COMMAND key (Macintosh) as you drag.

Guides Two straightedges—one horizontal and one vertical—for visually aligning objects. When an object is close to a guide, its corner or center, whichever is closer, snaps to the guide. You can think of a guide as having a "magnetic" attraction for objects; as objects get close to a guide, they seem to jump to it. You turn the guides on and off using the Guides command on the View menu. Drag a guide if you want to reposition it on your slide.

Stacking Placing objects on top of one another. Each object is separate from every other object as well as from the slide background. Although the objects seem to be drawn on a flat slide, it's helpful to think of objects as being like pieces of paper in a stack. The object you draw first is on the bottom of the stack; the most recently drawn object is added to the top of the stack. The "stacking order" is important because the object on the top of the stack can cover those underneath it. You can see this effect when you stack one filled object onto another filled object.

Multiple selection Selecting more than one object by holding down the SHIFT key and clicking the mouse button or by dragging a selection rectangle around the objects. When you flip, rotate, and resize a multiple selection, all objects in the multiple selection react independently.

Group A multiple selection that you treat as a single object by using the Group command on the Draw menu. Nested groups are multiple groups of objects, in a drawing, for example. Clip art often is built with nested groups.

Selecting and Grouping Objects

Objects are the basic units you use to create slides in PowerPoint. The box where you type text, the shapes you draw, even the pictures you bring in from other applications—all these are objects. You can have lots of objects on one slide.

Selecting and deselecting objects You need to tell PowerPoint which object (or objects) you want to work with. To do this, you click to select it. You select an object in a stack the same way. Once it's selected, you're free to add text to it, rotate it, change its shape, color, or pattern, or move it to another location. You can select multiple objects—just hold down the SHIFT key as you click the objects you want. To deselect a currently selected object, hold down the SHIFT key as you click the object you want to deselect.

Grouping objects   There will be times when you want to do the same thing to a number of objects. For instance, you may want to change the color of a series of shapes and then align them horizontally. Grouping objects combines them so you can work with them as if they were a single object. Once you've grouped objects, any attribute you choose is applied to all of the objects in the group. The objects all move, rotate, and flip as a group, too.

Grouping objects is the same as selecting multiple objects, with this exception: You can flip, rotate, and resize or scale all the objects in a group as a single unit, rather than having to move or change each object individually.

You can ungroup and regroup objects as you work. To regroup, you don't have to reselect each object as long as you haven't moved to another slide. Once objects have been grouped and ungrouped, the Regroup command on the Draw menu affects only the objects in the original group.

You can also create groups within groups—what we call nested groups. This is like creating a hierarchy of groups. Typically, you'd create a hierarchy of groups when drawing a complicated graphic. You'd draw one set of objects and then group them, draw the next set and group them, and so on. That way, if you need to redo any portion of the drawing, you can ungroup one set of objects without disturbing the others.

When you ungroup a nested group, PowerPoint ungroups it level by level. That is, if you select an object made up of nested groups and choose the Ungroup command, PowerPoint disassembles only the objects in the last group that was formed. Choose Ungroup again to disassemble the next group, and so on.

How to Select and Group Objects

Selecting or deselecting single objects

▶ **To select or deselect an object**

- To select an object, touch a visible part of the object with the pointer, and then click. To deselect a selected object, hold down the SHIFT key as you click the object you want to deselect.

  If the object you're selecting has no fill, click its border to select it. You know the object is selected when handles appear around it.

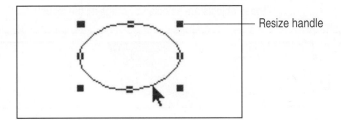

Resize handle

Select an unfilled object by clicking its border.

Tip You can use the TAB key to successively select all the objects on a slide beginning at the bottom of the slide until you reach the one you want. Pressing SHIFT+TAB cycles you through the objects beginning at the top of the slide.

Selecting or deselecting more than one object

▶ **To select or deselect more than one object**

- Click each object while pressing the SHIFT key.

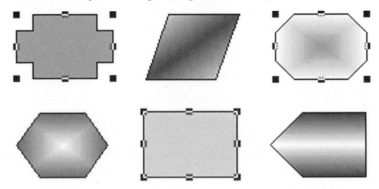

You can select or deselect noncontiguous objects by pressing the SHIFT key as you click each object.

As you select or deselect each object, any objects you've previously selected stay selected.

Tip You can select several contiguous objects by using your mouse to drag a selection rectangle around them.

These objects are selected by dragging the mouse.

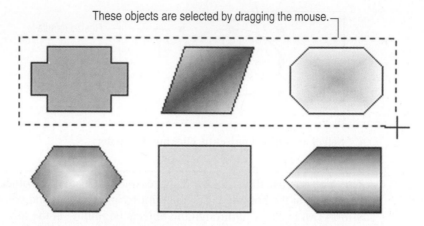

Drag the mouse to select objects that are next to each other.

Selecting all objects on a slide

▶ **To select all objects on a slide**

- From the Edit menu, choose Select All.

  −or−

  Press CTRL+A (Windows) or COMMAND+A (Macintosh).

For more information on selecting text, see "Selecting and Editing Text" in Chapter 4.

Grouping objects

Once you've selected two or more objects, you can create a group. Once you have a group any attribute you choose, such as shadow or line color, is assigned to all of the individual objects—as long as it applies. (You can't have a line with a shaded fill, for example.) The objects all move and rotate as a group, too.

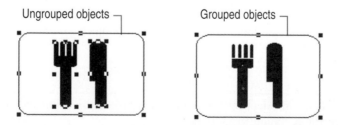

When you ungroup objects, you have the option of working with each object individually. Grouped objects let you apply attributes to all the objects at one time.

▶ **To group selected objects**

  ▪ From the Draw menu, choose Group.

    The handles for individual objects disappear, and handles appear for the
    selection rectangle that surrounds the group of objects.

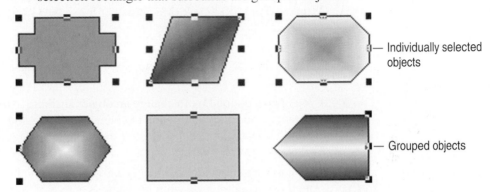
— Individually selected objects

— Grouped objects

**When you group objects, they lose their individual selection rectangles and resize
handles. You can always ungroup them to work with an individual object.**

  Now, anytime you click one of the objects, the group is selected.

Ungrouping objects

Let's say you've grouped some objects on a slide to move them or color them.
You can ungroup them again when you want to work with each object
individually.

▶ **To ungroup objects**

  1. Select the group by clicking one of its objects.
  2. From the Draw menu, choose Ungroup.

    Each object's handles appear; the group's resize handles disappear.

Regrouping objects

If you've grouped a set of objects and then ungrouped them, you can regroup
them.

▶ **To regroup objects**

  ▪ From the Draw menu, choose Regroup.

    The selection rectangle handles reappear around the most recently ungrouped
    group.

Hints for grouping, ungrouping, and regrouping objects

- A quick way to group and ungroup objects is to use the shortcut menu that appears when you select the group. Click the right mouse button (Windows) or CTRL+click (Macintosh). Or use the Group and Ungroup tools on the Drawing+ toolbar.

- To work with an individual object after you've ungrouped the objects, first click outside the group's selection rectangle to cancel the selection, and then click the object.

- If you open a dialog box to change an object attribute—for example, the Colors And Lines dialog box to change a color—and you don't see an option selected, it may be because the group of objects you've selected has a variety of fill colors.

- Be sure to regroup while the slide is active. PowerPoint remembers formerly grouped objects while the slide is active. If you switch to another slide and then come back and try to regroup, you'll have to select the objects, and then group them.

- Here's a shortcut for editing text in a single object in a group. Click the Text tool on the Drawing toolbar, and then click the text you want to edit. You don't have to ungroup the group.

- You can regroup without selecting every object first. If you choose the Regroup command, the most recently ungrouped group is reformed.

Moving and Aligning Objects

Naturally, you'll want to move objects around on your slides as you create a presentation. And sometimes you'll need to line up objects in a particular way—along the bottom of a slide, perhaps, or with each other.

Moving objects   You move objects differently depending on what kind they are and whether they have a fill. When you move a text object, click its selection box and drag. When you move an object that has a fill, click anywhere in the object and drag. To move an object that has no fill, click the border of the object and drag.

Aligning objects   There's an Align command that lets you choose the method of alignment you want to use. You can select all the objects you want to align, and then align them. Or you can use the horizontal and vertical rulers that are available in the PowerPoint window.

PowerPoint has a built-in reference system for aligning objects on slides. The system is made up of a grid and guides.

The grid is an invisible network of lines that covers the slide. There are 12 gridlines per inch and 5 gridlines per centimeter. As you draw objects, their corners align on the nearest intersection of the grid. Although you can't see the grid, it automatically helps align objects.

The guides are two straightedges, one horizontal and one vertical. You use the guides for aligning objects. When close to a guide, an object's corner or its center (whichever is closer) will snap to the guide. You can move the guides and create your own alignment. The guides are also handy for precise measurement of objects.

For in-depth procedures, in online Help see:

- Using the grid

- Using the guides

- Using the rulers

under "How to Move and Align Objects—In Depth" in the Chapter 3 Help Contents window.

How to Move and Align Objects

Moving objects

Here's how you move a text object, an object that you have created using the Drawing tools, and a picture.

▶ **To move an object**

1. Select the object. If the object is a drawn object or a picture, click its border to select it. If the object is filled, you can click anywhere within the object to select it.

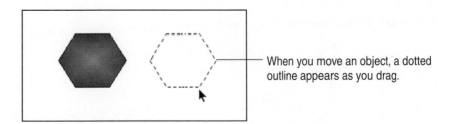

When you move an object, a dotted outline appears as you drag.

2. Drag the outline to its new location.

Moving a group of objects works the same way. Just click within the group and drag the entire group to a new location.

Tip You can place an object more precisely if it's not trying to snap to the grid. Press the ALT key (Windows) or the COMMAND key (Macintosh) as you drag or draw the object to temporarily turn off the grid.

Aligning objects

If you've created a group of objects, you can align the entire group on their left borders, their right borders, their top borders, their bottom borders, or their centers. You don't have to select and move each object individually.

▶ **To align objects**

1. Select the objects you want to align.

2. From the Draw menu, choose Align.

    The Align cascading menu appears.

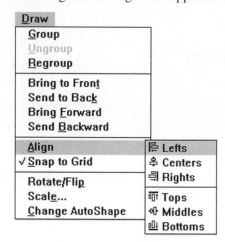

3. Select the type of alignment you want.

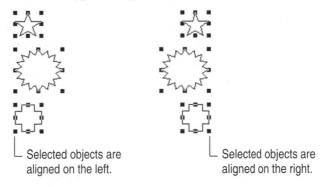

⌐ Selected objects are   ⌐ Selected objects are
  aligned on the left.   aligned on the right.

Tip Objects align according to their selection rectangles, not according to the shapes themselves.

Hints for moving and aligning objects

- You'll find toolbar buttons in the Customize Toolbars dialog box that can help you quickly align objects. Choose the Customize command on the Tools menu, and then, in the Categories box, select Arrange. You'll see a selection of buttons you can drag to the Custom toolbar or any other toolbar you find convenient. As you select each button, you'll find a short description of its function in the Description box.

- To use a guide to measure the distance from an arbitrary starting point, press the CTRL key (Windows) or the OPTION key (Macintosh) as you drag the guide.

- Pressing the SHIFT key while you move objects constrains them to horizontal or vertical movement.

- Objects are aligned according to their selection rectangles. For purposes of alignment, PowerPoint uses the selection rectangle that surrounds an object as the object's edge.

- Aligned objects aren't fixed in place. You can move any object out of alignment by dragging it.

- Freeform objects may not align the way you expect because PowerPoint sets their edges and centers according to their selection rectangles. You can always align them manually if their positioning doesn't please you. Use the guides and grid to help you.

Stacking Objects

When you're working with objects, you'll find that you sometimes stack them to get the effect you want. When you stack objects on top of each other, they overlap. Sometimes you'll want to change their order—put the top object on the bottom, for example.

Groups of objects can be stacked, too. You can move a group forward or backward in a stack.

You can use the TAB key to select an object buried in a stack.

PowerPoint has two sets of commands you can use to move objects up or down in a stack. You can move objects up or down one level at a time, or you can send an object all the way to the back or the front in one move. Having these commands means you don't have to keep track of the order of the objects as you draw them. That is, you don't have to draw the bottom object first, then the object that would be next on the stack, and so on. You can draw objects in any order and then move them up and down the stack as needed.

Here are some examples.

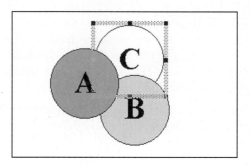
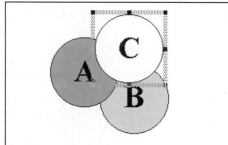

Select the object you want. Then choose the Bring To Front command. The object moves to the top of the stack.

How to Stack Objects

Bringing objects to the front and sending objects to the back of a stack

The Bring To Front and Send To Back commands move an object to the top and the bottom of a stack, respectively.

▶ **To bring an object to the front or send it to the back of a stack**

- Select the object you want to move and, from the Draw menu, choose Bring To Front or Send To Back.

Bringing an object forward one level or sending it back one level

The Bring Forward and Send Backward commands move an object up or down in the stack one level at a time.

▶ **To bring an object forward one level or send it back one level in a stack**

Say you have a stack of four objects and you want to move the top object down one level.

- Select the object you want to move and, from the Draw menu, choose Send Backward or Bring Forward.

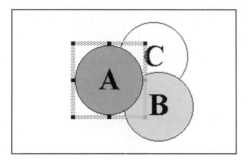 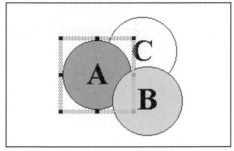

When you choose the Send Backward command, the selected object moves one level down.

Hints for stacking objects

- You'll find Bring To Front and Send To Back buttons in the Customize Toolbars dialog box in the Arrange category. You can use these to quickly move objects to the bottom or to the top of a stack.

- If you are uncertain of the stacking order you want, start by selecting an object, and then experiment with the Bring Forward and Send Backward commands.

- If you have a hard time grabbing an object in a stack, cycle through the objects by using the TAB key to go forward through the objects or SHIFT+TAB to go backward.

Rotating and Flipping Objects

You can rotate and flip any PowerPoint object, either one that is drawn in PowerPoint or one that you've converted to a PowerPoint object. Groups or multiple selections of objects can be rotated and flipped, too.

You can rotate to the left or right (90 degrees) and flip horizontally or vertically (180 degrees). Or you can rotate an object to the exact position you want by using the Free Rotate tool.

Note Most inserted pictures, graphs, organizational charts, and so on can't be rotated and flipped because they're not PowerPoint objects. If you can ungroup an inserted picture or chart, you can then regroup its objects into PowerPoint objects that can be rotated and flipped.

How to Rotate and Flip Objects

Flipping a selection

Flipping a selection turns an object or group of objects either horizontally or vertically.

You can change an object's point of reference by flipping it.

▶ **To flip an object or group**

1. Select the object or group of objects.

2. From the Draw menu, choose Rotate/Flip to display the Rotate/Flip cascading menu.

3. Choose Flip Horizontal or Flip Vertical. The object or group flips.

Tip You can flip or rotate an object that contains attached text. The text will rotate but will not flip. If you've added text using the Text tool, group the text and the object, and then flip or rotate them.

Rotating an object or group

You can rotate an object or group 90 degrees to the right or the left using the Rotate/Flip commands. For finer control of rotation, use the Free Rotation tool.

▶ **To rotate an object or group 90 degrees**

1. Select the object or group.

2. From the Draw menu, choose Rotate/Flip to display the Rotate/Flip cascading menu.

3. Choose Rotate Left or Rotate Right.

   The object or group rotates 90 degrees.

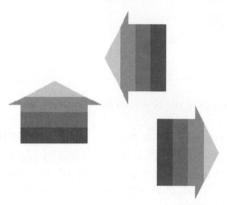

You use the Rotate Right and Rotate Left commands to rotate objects 90 degrees to the right or left.

Note   You cannot rotate or flip a group or selection that contains an imported picture.

Free-rotating an object or group

▶ **To free-rotate an object or group**

1. Select the object or group.

2. On the Drawing toolbar, click the Free Rotate tool.

   –or–

   Free Rotate tool

   From the Draw menu's Rotate/Flip cascading menu, click Free Rotate.

   The pointer changes into the Free Rotate pointer.

3. Position the Free Rotate pointer over a resize handle.

   The pointer becomes a four-arrow pointer. This pointer indicates that you can rotate the object in all four directions.

   Free Rotate pointer

4. Drag the handle until the outline of the selection is rotated to the position you want, and then release the mouse button.

Four-arrow pointer

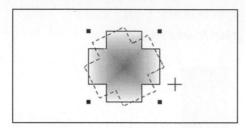

You can rotate by dragging the object to the right or left.

The status bar tells you how many degrees you've rotated the object.

The Free Rotate pointer remains available to you. If you need to, you can continue to adjust the amount of rotation without reselecting the Free Rotate tool. When you're finished, click anywhere on the slide, or click the Selection tool on the Drawing toolbar.

Free-rotating using the constraint keys

▶ **To free-rotate an object using constraint keys**

- To constrain the rotation to 45-degree increments, hold down the SHIFT key as you drag.

- To rotate the object around a resize handle, press the CTRL key, and then drag a handle opposite the handle you want to be the center of rotation.

- To constrain the rotation to 45-degree increments around a resize handle, press the SHIFT and CTRL keys as you drag.

Cutting, Copying, Pasting, and Duplicating Objects

The PowerPoint Cut, Copy, and Paste commands operate much the same as they do in other Microsoft applications. You can cut, copy, duplicate, and paste any PowerPoint object—text, shapes, pictures, or slides—using the commands from the Edit menu or the standard shortcut keys. The command names describe what they do:

Cut button

Copy button

- Cut—deletes an object and places it on the Clipboard so you can paste it elsewhere.

- Copy—makes a copy of an object and places it on the Clipboard.

- Paste—pastes the object from the Clipboard onto the slide, notes page, into a document in another application, and so on.

- Duplicate—makes a copy of an object and places it so it overlaps the original. Unlike the Copy command, Duplicate doesn't place a copy of the object on the Clipboard. You can use the Duplicate command to make an array of objects.

- Clear—deletes the object completely without putting a copy on the Clipboard.

Paste button

You'll find buttons for cutting, copying, and pasting on the Standard toolbar.

For in-depth procedures, in online Help see:

- Creating an array of objects

under "How to Cut, Copy, Paste, and Duplicate Objects—In Depth" in the Chapter 3 Help Contents window.

How to Cut, Copy, Paste, and Duplicate Objects

Cutting an object

When you cut an object, you delete it and place it on the Clipboard.

▶ **To cut an object**

1. Select the object.

2. From the Edit menu, choose Cut.

   The object disappears from the slide and is placed on the Clipboard.

Copying an object

Choosing the Copy command makes a copy of an object and places it on the Clipboard.

▶ **To copy an object**

1. Select the object.

2. From the Edit menu, choose Copy.

   The object you copied stays on the screen, and a copy of the object is stored on the Clipboard.

Pasting an object

Choosing the Paste command pastes the object on the Clipboard onto a slide, onto a notes page, into a document in another application, and so on. Once you've copied or cut an object, you can paste it.

▶ **To paste an object**

- From the Edit menu, choose Paste.

   The object appears on the slide, and you can move it to a new location.

You can paste the item as many times as you want until you copy another item to the Clipboard.

Duplicating an object

Duplicating an object creates a copy of the object that's slightly offset from the original. The Duplicate command *doesn't* place a copy of the object on the Clipboard. You can use the Duplicate command to make an array of objects.

Dragging is another way to duplicate an object. When you drag to duplicate, you don't place a copy on the Clipboard.

▶ **To duplicate an object**

1. Select the object or group.
2. From the Edit menu, choose Duplicate.

   The duplicate appears on top of the object(s) you are duplicating. Drag it to place it where you want it.

▶ **To duplicate an object by dragging**

1. Select the object.
2. Press the CTRL key (Windows) or the OPTION key (Macintosh) as you drag a copy of the object to its new location.

   When you press the CTRL key, a plus (+) sign appears next to the pointer.

Resizing Objects

You can change the size of an object by dragging one of the resize handles that surround a selected object.

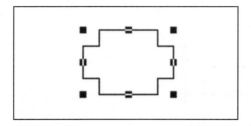

Resize handles appear around a selected object.

If you want to resize an object by an exact amount—by 50 percent, for example—use the Scale command on the Draw menu. To resize more than one object at a time, create a group, and then resize the group.

You can resize any PowerPoint object, as well as pictures, graphs, and other imported objects. You can easily maintain their original height-to-width ratio, or you can create interesting effects by distorting objects.

Depending on what kind of object you're resizing, the text within an object may or may not resize. If you've added text to an object you've drawn on the slide, the text won't resize. But if you're resizing an imported picture that includes text, the text will change size. Use the Scale command on the Draw menu to resize text in pictures so that the text doesn't get distorted.

You can resize individual objects, multiple selections, as well as groups.

For in-depth procedures, in online Help see:

- Scaling a selection

- Restoring the aspect ratio

under "How to Resize Objects—In Depth" in the Chapter 3 Help Contents window.

How to Resize Objects

Resizing an object
You can change the size and shape of an object by dragging its resize handles.

▶ **To resize an object**

1. Select the object.

2. Click a resize handle.

   The pointer changes to a cross-hair pointer.

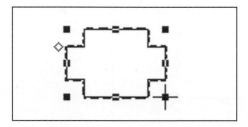

   The cross-hair pointer appears when you move the mouse pointer over a resize handle. It shows the direction in which you can resize the object.

3. Drag the cross-hair pointer until the outline of the object is the right shape and size.

Constraining while resizing an object

▶ **To constrain how objects move while you resize them**

- To resize an object vertically, horizontally, or diagonally from one corner. The diagonal resizing maintains the height-to-width relationship.
  - Windows: SHIFT + drag
  - Macintosh: SHIFT + drag
- To resize an object from the center outward.
  - Windows: CTRL + drag
  - Macintosh: OPTION + drag
- To resize an object vertically, horizontally, or diagonally from the center outward.
  - Windows: CTRL + SHIFT + drag
  - Macintosh: OPTION + SHIFT+ drag

Resizing a line

▶ **To resize a line**

1. Select the line.

   Resize handles appear on each end of the line.

2. Drag one of the resize handles to make the line the length you want.

To lengthen and reposition a line, grab a resize handle and drag. You'll see an image of the resized line as you drag.

Hold down the SHIFT key to resize a line without changing its position.

You can also change the position of the line as you drag—the end you aren't dragging remains anchored; the end you are dragging can be repositioned, extended, or shortened.

If you want to make sure the line stays at the same angle while you resize it, press SHIFT while resizing.

Enhancing Objects

PowerPoint objects have attributes that define how the objects appear on a slide. The attributes are:

- Line—the border around an object
- Fill—the color that fills the inside of an object
- Shadow—the shadow of an object

Of course, a line can exist on its own, without serving as a border for an object. Lines and borders have similar attributes. Lines, arcs, and freeform shapes can have arrowheads, though, while borders can't.

PowerPoint objects come with a defined set of attributes—default settings that are taken from the presentation's Slide Master. The default settings are automatically available when you use one of the toolbar buttons to assign an attribute. For example, use the Apply Fill Defaults button on the Drawing toolbar to apply the default fill color; use the Colors And Lines command on the Format menu or the Fill Color tool on the Drawing+ toolbar to choose a different fill color.

You can change the default settings as you like. That's part of the fun of working with PowerPoint.

Finally, there's the Format Painter tool. If you create an object with just the right border, fill color, and so on, you can "pick up" all the attributes of that object and apply them to another object, using the Format Painter tool.

For in-depth procedures, in online Help, see:

- Adjusting the amount of shadow offset

- Adding an embossed effect to an object

- Changing defaults

under "How to Enhance Objects—In Depth" in the Chapter 3 Help Contents window.

Tip   You can create a Custom toolbar that incorporates the tools you like to use in creating colorful objects. It's easy to drag the toolbar buttons you want from the Customize Toolbars dialog box to a toolbar.

How to Enhance Objects

PowerPoint provides many features—such as borders, object fills, and shadows —to help you make your slides more dynamic.

Working with borders

When you put a border around an object, you add a line to it that defines its shape. PowerPoint automatically adds a thin border to any object you draw. You can also add borders to text boxes, to pictures, and to artwork you've imported into your presentation.

You can also choose to delete a border, or you can change its style—you can make a dotted or dashed border, you can color a border, and you can pick a border weight.

The Colors And Lines command on the Format menu gives you access to all the border styles. You'll be able to make several choices at once and then preview your changes before accepting the border style.

Here's the Colors And Lines dialog box.

Choose line styles here. ┐   ┌ Choose dashed lines here.

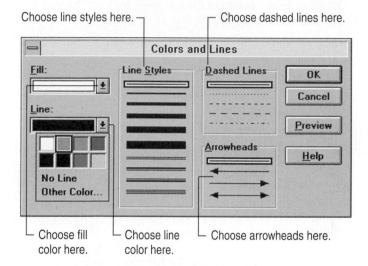

└ Choose fill   └ Choose line   └ Choose arrowheads here.
  color here.   color here.

You might find it handy, too, to use the buttons on the Drawing and Drawing+ toolbars to make quick changes to borders.

Here are the buttons you'll most often use in working with borders.

These tools are on
┌ the Drawing+ toolbar.

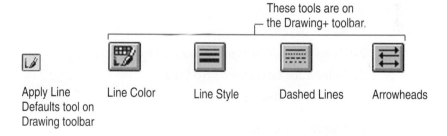

Apply Line   Line Color   Line Style   Dashed Lines   Arrowheads
Defaults tool on
Drawing toolbar

Use the Apply Line Defaults tool on the Drawing toolbar to toggle a line on and off. Use the tools on the Drawing+ toolbar to change the appearance of a line.

Tip   You can make simple changes to borders by using the toolbar buttons. But if you want to experiment with all the border options, use the Colors And Lines command on the Format menu.

Adding borders

▶ **To add a border**

1. Select the object and, from the Format menu, choose Colors And Lines.

    The Colors And Lines dialog box appears.

2. In the Line Styles box, select the type of line you want.

    You can select dotted or dashed lines for your border, as well as the weight of the line and the color.

    Here are some objects with different borders.

    Using different line styles, weights, and colors can add visual interest to AutoShapes.

3. In the Line box, choose a color for your border.

4. Choose OK.

    The border you have chosen appears around the object.

Removing borders

▶ **To remove a border**

1. Select the object.

2. From the Format menu, choose Colors And Lines.

3. In the Line box, choose No Line.

    The border disappears.

Changing borders

▶ **To change a border**

1. Select the object that has the border you want to change.

2. From the Format menu, choose Colors And Lines.

3. Make the changes you want in the Colors And Lines dialog box and choose OK.

    You can choose Preview to see your changes before you accept them. You can move the dialog box if it's in your way.

Working with object fills

The interiors of objects can be filled with solid colors, two-color patterns, shaded colors, or the same color or shade as the background of the slide.

When you fill an object, it becomes opaque. You can also choose to create objects with no fill, thus making them transparent.

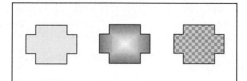 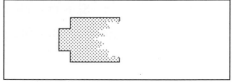

Here are some of the effects you can create using object fills. Fill an object with the background color and use it to mask other objects.

Objects are filled as you draw them if the Fill box in the Colors And Lines dialog box is set to Shaded, to Patterned, or to a specific color. If the Fill box is set to No Fill, the object isn't filled.

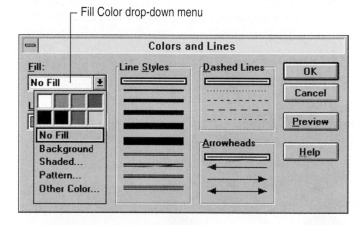

You can change fill colors and line styles, add arrowheads, and shade an object in one dialog box.

You can also use the toolbar shortcuts on the Drawing and Drawing+ toolbars to add, remove, or change the fill of objects.

The Apply Fill   The Fill Color
Defaults tool on the   tool on the
Drawing toolbar   Drawing+ toolbar

Filling an object with the default fill color

▶ **To fill an object with the default fill color**

1. Select the object.

2. Click the Apply Fill Defaults tool on the Drawing toolbar.

   The object is filled with the color and becomes opaque.

Tip   You can fill several objects at the same time by using the SHIFT key to select them and then clicking the Apply Fill Defaults tool on the Drawing toolbar.

Filling an object with other colors

▶ **To fill an object with a color other than the default fill color**

1. Select the object.

2. From the Format menu, choose Colors And Lines.

   The Colors And Lines dialog box appears.

3. In the Fill box, select the color you want.

   You can click Preview to see your changes before you accept them. You can move the dialog box if it's in your way.

Shading the fill color

Shading the color in an object creates a dynamic 3-D effect. Any PowerPoint object can be filled with a shaded color.

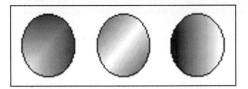

You can vary the effect of shaded fills to create the illusion of different textures and different light sources.

▶ **To shade the fill color in an object**

1. Select the object you want to shade.

2. From the Format menu, choose Colors And Lines.

   The Colors And Lines dialog box appears.

3. In the Fill drop-down box, choose Shaded.

The Shaded Fill dialog box appears.

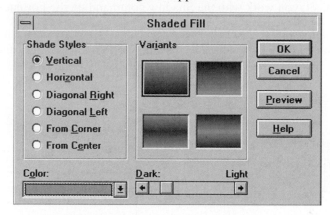

Select the shading style and variant you like.

4. Choose a color for your shaded object in the Color box.

5. Choose the style of shading you want.

As you select a style, such as Diagonal Right or Diagonal Left, the variations available to you appear in the Variants box on the right.

6. Move the scroll bar to make the shading darker or lighter.

As you move the scroll bar, you again see the effect in the Variants box.

7. In the Variants box, select the variant that most appeals to you.

8. Choose OK when you've found the effect you want.

9. Choose OK in the Colors And Lines dialog box.

Removing fill

▶ **To remove a fill**

1. Select an object from which you want to remove a fill.

2. From the Format menu, choose Colors And Lines.

3. In the Fill box, select No Fill.

4. Choose OK.

The fill is removed from the selected object.

Tip You can quickly remove an object's fill by clicking the Apply Fill Defaults tool on the Drawing toolbar. Remember that the Apply Fill Defaults tool always uses the default fill color to fill objects.

Working with shadows

You can shadow or emboss PowerPoint objects. When you shadow or emboss an object, you work with the Shadow command on the Format menu.

Shadows give a 3-D effect to objects and make them appear to float on the slide. You can adjust the amount of shadow offset to create just the right effect.

You can adjust the direction and amount of shadow offset to create different 3-D effects.

Embossing is similar to shadowing an object, except it uses extra highlighting to produce the effect. Because of the way the eye perceives embossing and colors, embossing looks best on objects that are the same color as the slide background. Therefore, when you emboss a filled object, PowerPoint makes the object the same color as the background. You can restore the object's color if you want to. Experiment for interesting effects—try different combinations of borders and fill.

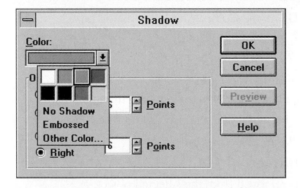

Choose a new shadow color or emboss objects using the Shadow dialog box and Color drop-down box.

You can also use the toolbar commands to add and remove shadows and to change the shadow color.

The Apply Shadow   The Shadow Color
Defaults tool on the   tool on the
Drawing toolbar   Drawing+ toolbar

Note Embossing does not work well on either a black or a white background.

Adding the default shadow

▶ **To add a shadow using the default shadow color**

- To apply the color that's already assigned for shadowing objects, click the Apply Shadow tool on the Drawing toolbar.

Adding a shadow with nondefault colors

▶ **To add a shadow with a color other than the default shadow color**

1. Select the object.

   Make sure the object you want to shadow has a border or is filled with a color other than the slide's background color. Otherwise, your shadowed object will lack definition.

2. From the Format menu, choose Shadow.

   The Shadow dialog box appears.

3. In the Color box, select the color of the shadow you want for the object.

4. Choose OK.

Removing a shadow

▶ **To remove a shadow**

1. Select the shadowed object.

2. From the Format menu, choose Shadow.

   The Shadow dialog box appears.

3. In the Color drop-down box, select No Shadow.

Working with the Format Painter

You can quickly change the appearance of an object by copying the attributes (color, shadow, pattern, and so on) of another object whose appearance you like. You can then apply these attributes directly to the object you want to change. The Format Painter can be used with objects and their attributes, but not with graphs and pictures.

▶ **To pick up and apply style using the Format Painter**

1. Select the object whose attributes you want to copy.

2. Click the Format Painter button on the Standard toolbar.

Format Painter button

The pointer changes to a paint brush.

3. Click inside the object to which you want to apply the attributes.

    The selected object takes on its new attributes.

Filling objects with a pattern

Objects can be filled with two-color patterns. You can assign colors to the background and to the foreground of a pattern.

▶ **To fill an object with a pattern**

1. Select an object that can be filled.

2. From the Format menu, choose Colors And Lines.

3. In the Fill drop-down box, choose Pattern.

   The Pattern Fill dialog box appears.

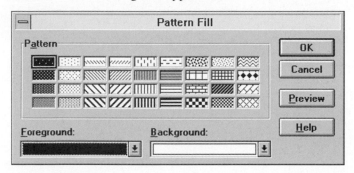

   You can change the look of a pattern by reversing the foreground and the background colors.

4. In the Pattern Fill dialog box, choose the following:

   ▪ a pattern,

   ▪ a pattern foreground color (a color for the pattern elements), and

   ▪ a pattern background color.

5. To preview the selected pattern on your slide, click Preview.

   The selected object is filled with the pattern. (You may have to move the dialog box to see the object.)

6. Choose OK to confirm the pattern and apply it to the selected object. Then choose OK in the Colors And Lines dialog box.

C H A P T E R   4

Putting Text on Slides

In this chapter, you'll find some ideas about working with text. You'll find explanations of typing text—on slides, in shapes, and using the Text tool. You'll see how to edit text in PowerPoint—how to cut, duplicate, copy, and paste. You'll also learn about formatting text and paragraphs. In the final section, there's an introduction to working with outlines, followed by procedures you use to create and work with your outlines in PowerPoint.

In This Chapter

Typing Text

In general, typing text is as simple as clicking and typing. When there's a text placeholder on your slide, just click inside it and you're ready to add your text.

The format of the text on the Slide Master determines how it looks on the slide—how it's aligned, what font is used, whether it's italic, and so on. The title and each level of text have their own formats on the Slide Master.

For more information on working with the Slide Master, see Chapter 2, "Creating Presentations and Slides."

To add text outside a text placeholder, use the Text tool on the Drawing toolbar.

After you've typed your text, you can edit and format it to get the look you want.

Terms That Apply to Typing Text

Here are some terms that apply when you're typing text:

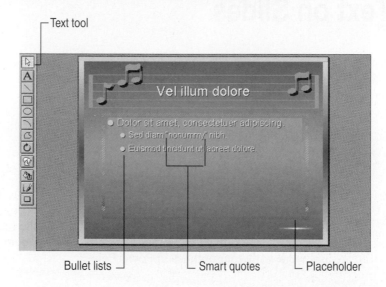

Placeholders **Placeholders** Boxes appear on a slide before you type anything. These are called placeholders. Each placeholder is surrounded by a dotted line. Some are specifically formatted to contain text. In these placeholders, you'll find a message telling you to click and type your text. However, you can add text to any placeholder. Text that you type in the title and main text placeholders appears in your outline.

Paragraph A paragraph is defined as text that begins when you press ENTER (Windows) or RETURN (Macintosh) and ends when you press ENTER or RETURN again. When you align text and add bullets, these attributes apply to paragraphs. When you work on paragraphs, you can set tabs and indents, adjust your line and paragraph spacing, and set the alignment for text in the paragraph.

Text tool You can use the Text tool, which is on the Drawing toolbar, to add text anywhere on a slide. Click the Text tool to select it, and then just click and start typing, or drag a text box to automatically wordwrap your text and then start typing. Text that you type with the Text tool doesn't appear in Outline view.

Bullet lists Text placeholders on some AutoLayouts are set up to create bullet lists for you automatically. All you do is click and type. When you press ENTER, a new bullet is added so you can type the next item on the list. You can change the look of the bullets—the style, color, and placement—using menu commands and toolbar buttons or you can turn a bullet off for an item on a list.

Smart quotes Smart quotes are the quotation marks used by typesetters. They're curly, and opening quotation marks and closing quotation marks differ from each other. (To turn smart quotes on or off, just change the preferences using the Options command on the Tools menu.)

How to Type Text

Typing text on a slide

Each new slide you create contains placeholders. Depending on the AutoLayout you select, you may have a placeholder for the slide title as well as the main text.

The easiest way to add text to slides is to type in the text placeholders that appear on most AutoLayouts. Usually there is a placeholder for a title and one or more for text and objects.

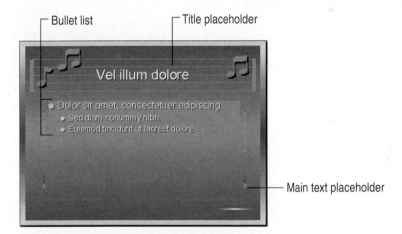

You can change slide layouts if you want different placeholders. Use the Layout button on the status bar.

For in-depth procedures, in online Help see:

- Inserting special characters

under "How to Type Text—In Depth" in the Chapter 4 Help Contents window.

▶ **To type a slide title**

1. Click the placeholder labeled "Click to add title."

   The placeholder title disappears, and an insertion point takes its place.

2. Start typing your text.

▶ **To type text on a slide**

- Click the placeholder labeled "Click to add text" and start typing.

  When you press ENTER (Windows) or RETURN (Macintosh), you create a new paragraph at the same level. You can use the TAB key, shortcut keys, and the Promote and Demote buttons on the Formatting toolbar to create indent levels and move paragraphs around.

Tip You can add a text placeholder to a slide if you've deleted it. Click the Layout button on the status bar, and then choose Reapply in the Slide Layout dialog box to reapply the layout you started with.

Typing Text in Shapes

Rectangles, circles, triangles, and other closed shapes drawn with the AutoShapes tools can have text attached to them. After drawing a shape, just start typing. Your text is automatically centered in the object.

The way text fits into a shape depends on the setting in the Text Anchor dialog box. Check the Adjust Object Size To Fit Text check box to resize the object to fit around the text. (If that check box is not selected and you resize the object, text may run over the edges.) You can also align the text in different ways—on the left or right margins, vertically, and so on.

For in-depth procedures, in online Help see:

- Setting the anchor point for text within a shape
- Adjusting an object's size to fit text
- Making text wrap in an object
- Changing the margins around text in a shape

under "How to Type Text in Shapes—In Depth" in the Chapter 4 Help Contents window.

Anchor point	Direction of text growth

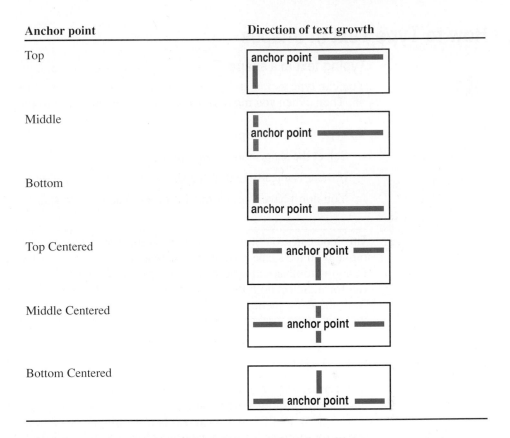

Top	
Middle	
Bottom	
Top Centered	
Middle Centered	
Bottom Centered	

The blue lines in this illustration indicate the directions in which additional text expands.

When you drag to resize a shape that contains text, the size of the text doesn't change automatically. To change it, select the text and change the font size by clicking the arrow next to the Font Size box on the Formatting toolbar.

When you type in a shape, PowerPoint treats the text as part of the shape. When you move the shape, the text moves with it.

How to Type Text in Shapes

Text tool

Typing text in a shape

You can type text in any closed AutoShape—rectangles, stars, triangles, and so on. Then, when you move or rotate the shape, the text will move with it.

▶ **To type text in a shape**

- Select the shape and begin typing.

  If there is already text in the shape, the new text is added at the end.

  You don't have to click the Text tool to add text to shapes.

Tip You can group lines, arcs, and freeform objects with text so the text will move with the shape, just as if it were attached. Select the Text tool on the Drawing toolbar and type your text. Then position the text next to the line, arc, or freeform. Select both the text and the shape, and then choose the Group command from the Draw menu.

Using the Text Tool

You can use the Text tool whenever you want to add text other than a slide title or main text to a slide. When you type using the Text tool, you can choose to have text wrap or not. If you draw a text box, wordwrap is automatically on. To add text—for example, to add a caption below a graphic—select the Text tool, click the slide and begin typing.

Text boxes have a shape. If you add a border using the Apply Line Color toolbar button, your text appears in a rectangle. You can change the rectangle to any AutoShape, using the Change AutoShape command on the Draw menu.

If you resize an object that contains attached text, the text remains its original size. If you want to make the text larger or smaller, select it and change the font size. To make the shape and the text resize as one, use the Scale command on the Draw menu.

Text created with the Text tool does not appear in Outline view.

How to Use the Text Tool

Adding a caption using the Text tool

By default, text typed with the Text tool doesn't wrap, unless you drag a text box. If you just click and don't drag, the line of text will get longer as you type.

▶ **To add a caption using the Text tool**

- Select the Text tool, and then click and type wherever you want to add the caption.

Making text wordwrap

There are times when you'll want to constrain the text you type with the Text tool to a certain width. This means having the text wrap so it stays within the width you've established.

▶ **To make text wrap using the Text tool**

1. Select the Text tool and drag a box on the slide where you want to add text.

   Make the box the approximate width of the text you're adding.

2. Begin typing.

   As you type, the text wraps in the text box you drew.

3. Resize the box after you've typed your text if you want.

   The text will continue to wrap inside the box.

Tip   You can always change the wordwrap behavior of text using the Text Anchor command on the Format menu.

Selecting and Editing Text

The first step in editing text is to select it so PowerPoint knows which text you're working on. If you've used any of the standard word-processing programs, such as Microsoft Word, you already know about selecting text for editing. PowerPoint follows most of the procedures you're familiar with and adds a few to make text selection easier.

Terms That Apply to Selecting and Editing Text

Automatic word selection   This selection option makes it easier to select multiple words. Rather than having to place the pointer precisely at the beginning of the first word you want to select and then drag to the end of the last word, you just make sure the pointer is within the first word, and then drag to anywhere in the last word. PowerPoint automatically selects the entire first and last words for you.

Insertion point selection   You can make changes to a word—italicize it or change its font style, for instance—without going to the trouble of highlighting it. Just place the pointer between two letters of the word and make the changes you want, using the menu commands.

Smart Cut and Paste When you use the Cut and Paste commands for text, the Smart Cut and Paste feature makes sure the words are correctly spaced. To turn this option off in PowerPoint, use the Options command on the Tools menu.

Checking spelling There's a spelling checker available that checks the spelling throughout your presentation. The spelling checker doesn't check words in pictures or other imported objects, however. You'll need to check them in their original application.

Find and replace text If you decide to change a word throughout your presentation, you can find it and replace it with another using the Find and Replace commands. These commands don't work for text in pictures and imported objects. The search covers the entire presentation—slides, outlines, speaker's notes, and audience handouts.

How to Select and Edit Text

Selecting text using keyboard shortcuts

For keyboard enthusiasts, selecting text using the keyboard is often faster than using the mouse. PowerPoint has a complete set of key combinations for selecting text to edit.

▶ **To select text using keyboard shortcuts**

Here's a summary of the keys and what they do.

Keyboard Shortcuts for Selecting Text

To move	Press (Windows)	Press (Macintosh)
One character right	SHIFT+RIGHT ARROW	SHIFT+RIGHT ARROW
One character left	SHIFT+LEFT ARROW	SHIFT+LEFT ARROW
To end of word	CTRL+SHIFT+RIGHT ARROW	COMMAND+RIGHT ARROW
To beginning of word	CTRL+SHIFT+LEFT ARROW	COMMAND+LEFT ARROW
One line up	SHIFT+UP ARROW	SHIFT+UP ARROW
One line down	SHIFT+DOWN ARROW	SHIFT+DOWN ARROW
Select all objects on slide	CTRL+A	COMMAND+A
Select all text in an object (text edit mode)	CTRL+A	COMMAND+A
Select all text (Outline view)	CTRL+A	COMMAND+A

Moving text using the mouse

You can select text and then drag and move it to a new place within an object on a slide or anywhere in your outline. It works just as it does in Microsoft Word.

▶ **To move text using the mouse (drag and drop)**

1. Select the text you want to move.

2. Drag the text to its new location as you hold the mouse button down.

   As you move, a box appears at the bottom of the pointer, and a small dotted line follows your pointer to show you where the text will be placed when you release the mouse button.

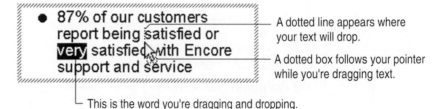

87% of our customers report being satisfied or **very** satisfied with Encore support and service

A dotted line appears where your text will drop.

A dotted box follows your pointer while you're dragging text.

This is the word you're dragging and dropping.

3. When the text is where you want it, release the mouse button.

   The selected text moves to its new location.

Copying and pasting text using the mouse

You can use the Selection tool to copy text, and then drag the copy to a new location.

▶ **To copy text and paste it using the mouse**

1. Select the text you want to copy and move.

2. Hold down the CTRL key (Windows) or the OPTION key (Macintosh) while you drag the text to a new location on the slide.

   You'll see a plus sign next to the pointer while you're dragging, as well as a dotted line to show you where the copy will be placed.

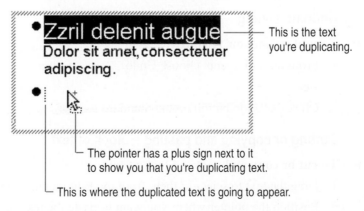

Zzril delenit augue
Dolor sit amet, consectetuer adipiscing.

This is the text you're duplicating.

The pointer has a plus sign next to it to show you that you're duplicating text.

This is where the duplicated text is going to appear.

Adding text to a text placeholder

▶ **To add text to a text placeholder**

- Click inside a text placeholder, and start typing.

  If you've already added text to the placeholder, position the I-beam pointer at the point where you want to begin, click and then start typing.

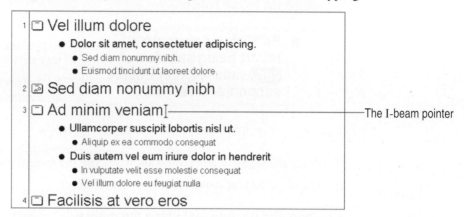

The I-beam pointer

Deleting text

▶ **To delete a character**

- Position the pointer after the character you want to delete, click and then press BACKSPACE (Windows) or DELETE (Macintosh).

▶ **To delete a block of text**

- Drag across the text to highlight it, and press BACKSPACE (Windows) or DELETE (Macintosh), or type the replacement text.

Undoing editing

▶ **To undo what you've edited**

- From the Edit menu, choose Undo.

  −or−

  Click the Undo button on the Standard toolbar.

Cutting or copying and pasting a block of text

▶ **To cut or copy and paste a block of text**

1. Drag the text to select it; then, from the Edit menu, choose Cut or Copy.
2. Position the pointer where you want to paste the text and click.
3. With text on the Clipboard (cut or copied), from the Edit menu, choose Paste.

How to Find and Replace Text

Finding text

PowerPoint can find any word or phrase in a presentation except for those in embedded objects (in charts, for example).

▶ **To find text**

1. From the Edit menu, choose Find.

2. Type the text you want to find in the Find What box.

3. At the bottom of the dialog box are check boxes for matching whole words or the case—that is, uppercase and lowercase—of characters. Select those check boxes if you want to focus your search.

4. Choose the Find Next button.

   If PowerPoint finds the word or phrase in your presentation, the text will be highlighted. Choose the Find Next button each time to continue the search.

   You can drag the dialog box out of the way so it doesn't cover the text.

5. When you finish searching, choose the Close button.

Tip You can create a presentation containing commonly used slides, including keywords for each of the notes pages. Then use the Find command in Slide Sorter view to find just the slides you want. In Slide Sorter view, Find Next changes to Find All, and all slides containing the keyword will be selected. You can then drag and drop those slides into another presentation.

Finding and replacing text

You can find a word and replace it with a new word or phrase. For example, you can use the Find and Replace commands to find every instance of "Mr. Smith" and replace it with "Mr. Smythe." Or you can find and replace a phrase such as "first quarter 1994" with "third quarter 1994." This is particularly helpful when updating slides from an earlier presentation.

▶ **To find and replace text**

1. From the Edit menu, choose Replace.

   The Replace dialog box appears.

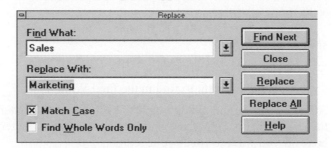

   Select the Match Case check box when you want to narrow your search to uppercase or lowercase versions of the word or phrase.

2. Type the text you want to find in the Find What box.

3. Press TAB or click in the Replace With box and type the text you want for the replacement.

   For example, to replace all instances of "Smith" with "Smythe," type **Smith** in the Find What box and type **Smythe** in the Replace With box.

4. At the bottom of the dialog box are check boxes for matching whole words or case.

   - **Match Case**—finds only those words that match the capitalization of the Find word or words.

   - **Find Whole Words Only**—finds and replaces only whole words. For example, if you want to replace "Smith" with "Smythe," PowerPoint won't highlight "Smithy" if this box is selected.

5. Choose the appropriate button, depending on what you want to do:

   - **Find Next**—continues to search the presentation to find the next instance of the text. The text is selected but not yet changed. Use this option when you're not sure whether you want to change the text.

   - **Replace**—changes the selected text and then finds the next instance of that text but doesn't change it. Use this option when you're sure you want to change the selected text but not sure whether you want to change its next instance.

   - **Replace All**—changes every instance of the text. To interrupt the process, press ESC (Windows) or COMMAND+PERIOD (Macintosh).

6. When you finish searching and replacing, choose the Close button.

Hints on finding and replacing text

- You can go directly to the Replace dialog box from the Find dialog box by choosing the Replace button in the Find dialog box.

- To find a different word or phrase after you've found and replaced one word or phrase, enter a new one in the Find What box and repeat the process.

- If you remember, for example, that a slide has the phrase "Top sales performers" and you want to find that slide, you can search for the phrase using the Find command instead of manually searching through the presentation.

How to Check Spelling

Checking spelling in a presentation

The spelling checker checks the spelling in the entire presentation—all slides, the outline, the notes pages, and the handout pages. PowerPoint starts by using its main dictionary to check spelling and then lets you open a custom dictionary.

You don't have to select any text to check a presentation's spelling. You only need to open the presentation and then tell PowerPoint to check the spelling.

▶ **To check the spelling in a presentation**

1. From the Tools menu, choose Spelling.

   −or−

   Click the Spelling button on the Standard toolbar.

PowerPoint opens the main dictionary and the available custom dictionaries to check the spelling.

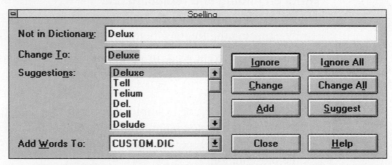

You can add words to the custom dictionary by choosing the Add button when the word appears in the Not In Dictionary box.

PowerPoint then checks the spelling, starting at the current location in the presentation.

2. When PowerPoint doesn't recognize a word, it appears in the Not In Dictionary box. You have a number of choices:

   - **Manually correct the word**—You can just retype the word in the Change To box, and then choose Change.

     If you want to change any subsequent occurrences of the same misspelling, choose Change All. If you only want to change the one occurrence, choose Change.

   - **Pick one of the suggested alternatives**—PowerPoint lists possible correct spellings for the word in the Suggestions box. Scroll through the list, find the word you want, select it, and choose Change or Change All.

   - **Ignore the misspelling**—Choose Ignore when the word is spelled correctly but it's not in the dictionary (such as a proper name or an obscure scientific term). Choosing Ignore does not add it to a custom dictionary, and PowerPoint will tell you it doesn't recognize the word each time you check the presentation's spelling.

     If you click Ignore All, PowerPoint then ignores that word anywhere it appears in the presentation.

   - **Add**—When you choose Add, PowerPoint adds the word to a custom dictionary.

     Your choices of custom dictionaries are listed in the Add Words To box. If you've created additional custom dictionaries, you need only choose the one you want to use.

3. When you've checked your entire presentation, a message appears telling you that PowerPoint is finished checking your presentation. Choose OK to exit the spelling checker.

Using a custom dictionary

PowerPoint shares a custom dictionary with other Microsoft applications. In other words, any custom dictionary that you use with any Microsoft product—Word, for example—you can also use with PowerPoint. A custom dictionary is where you'd store names, cities, products, acronyms, and so on—words that aren't part of the standard dictionary. Any custom dictionary you use with your other Microsoft applications will also work with PowerPoint.

Note   You can add words to a custom dictionary in PowerPoint, but you can't remove words.

Hints on checking spelling

- Text in embedded objects won't be checked. If you import a picture that contains text, PowerPoint isn't able to check it because that text is treated as part of the image.

- The main dictionary contains commonly used English words. It doesn't contain long technical terms, poetic contractions (such as "e'er"), or archaic terms. The spelling checker will treat those words as though they are misspelled. You can have PowerPoint either ignore them or add them to a custom dictionary.

- You can make the spelling checker faster by clearing Spelling: Always Suggest. From the Tools menu, choose Options, and then clear the Spelling: Always Suggest check box.

- In Windows, Microsoft applications can all use the same custom dictionary as long as it is stored in the shared MS® directory and recorded in the WIN.INI file. If you've already created one for Microsoft Word, for example, PowerPoint will add your special words to that same custom dictionary. If you have more than one custom dictionary, choose the one you want in the Add Words To box.

- On the Macintosh, Microsoft applications can all use the same custom dictionary as long as it is stored in the Microsoft Spelling folder. If you have more than one custom dictionary, you can choose the one you want in the dictionary drop-down list.

Formatting Text

How your text looks depends on the attributes you assign to it. (Think of an attribute as a characteristic of the text—its font, size, color, whether it's italic or boldface, and so on.)

Style	Examples of text attributes
Plain	International sales fueling sales growth
Underlined	International sales fueling sales growth
Bold	**International sales fueling sales growth**
Italic	*International sales fueling sales growth*
Shadowed	International sales fueling sales growth
Superscript	ENCORE™
Subscript	H_2SO_4

You can use the commands on the Format menu to change text attributes, or you can use the tools on the Formatting toolbar to change the font and font size and its attributes (italic, bold, underlined, or shadowed).

Text within shapes can also be embossed, superscripted, and subscripted.

You can change the format for the title or body text for your entire presentation by changing the title or text format on the Slide Master.

For in-depth procedures, in online Help see:

- Using smart quotes
- Changing case
- Adding or deleting periods
- Changing the bullet style

under "How to Format Text—In Depth" in the Chapter 4 Help Contents window.

Terms That Apply to Formatting Text

Formatting toolbar The Formatting toolbar is available in Slide, Outline, and Notes views. The tools on this toolbar give you quick access to some of the attributes you commonly apply to text. If the toolbar is hidden, you can display it using the Toolbars command on the View menu.

Text attributes Any characteristic, such as font, font size, style, color, subscript, or superscript, is an attribute of that text. You can adjust text attributes before, during, or after you type the text.

Text rulers   When you display the text rulers, they appear on the left and at the top of the PowerPoint window. Click in a placeholder or an object to see the margins and tabs that apply to that placeholder or object. When you click text in an object, you see the horizontal ruler change to show your margins and tabs. You can use the horizontal ruler to set your tabs and adjust margins for text objects.

Applying a format from one text object to another   If you find a text format you like, you can pick up and apply that format to another text object, using the Format Painter button or the Pick Up and Apply Style commands.

How to Format Text

Changing text attributes

The tools on the Formatting toolbar and the Font command on the Format menu give you access to all sorts of text styles. You can change the color of your text, its size, font, and so on.

Here's the Font dialog box.

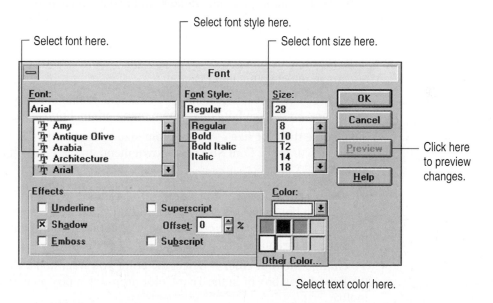

The current font and its attributes are highlighted. If you want to preview changes, click Preview. You can move the Font dialog box if it's in your way by dragging the title bar.

You'll also find it convenient to use the tools on the PowerPoint Formatting toolbar. You can make all sorts of quick changes to your text with a click of the mouse.

Here's the Formatting toolbar.

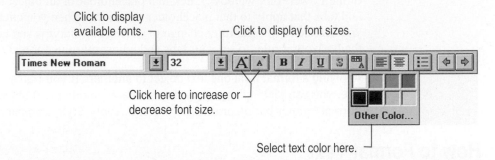

Clicking the text editing buttons on the Formatting toolbar toggles an attribute on and off.

▶ **To change the attributes of text**

1. Select the text you want to change.

2. Choose a tool on the Formatting toolbar, and make the changes you want to the text.

   −or−

   From the Format menu, choose Font, and then use the options in the Font dialog box to make your changes.

   ▪ **To change the font**—Select the font you want in the Font box in the Font dialog box, or use the Font drop-down menu on the Formatting toolbar.

   ▪ **To change the font size**—Select a font size in the Size box in the Font dialog box or in the Font Size drop-down menu on the Formatting toolbar.

   You can also click in the Size box and type the size you want.

   ▪ **To change the font style (bold and italic)**—In the Font Style box in the Font dialog box, choose the styles you want from the available font styles. On the Formatting toolbar, click a button or combination of buttons to get the style you want.

   ▪ **To change the font color**—Select the color you want in the Color box in the Font dialog box or in the Text Color drop-down box on the Formatting toolbar.

   If you don't see the color you want, choose Other Color, and then pick a new color in the Other Color dialog box.

3. If you're working in the Font dialog box, choose OK.

Tip **Tip** You can use the Increase Font Size and the Decrease Font Size buttons on the Formatting toolbar to increase and decrease font sizes in a multiple selection that includes different font sizes. With each click of the button, all the fonts in a selection increase or decrease by about 10 percent.

Shadowing and embossing text

Shadowing adds a drop shadow behind your text for emphasis. Embossing text is somewhat like shadowing it, except the effect is one of a highlight rather than a shadow. The embossed text becomes the same color as the background, and it appears to be raised slightly.

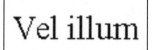

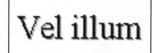

Regular text   Shadowed text   Embossed text

▶ **To shadow text**

1. Select the text you want to shadow.

2. On the Formatting toolbar, click the Shadow tool.

   –or–

   From the Format menu, choose Font.

   The Font dialog box appears.

3. In the Effects box, select Shadow.

4. Choose OK.

▶ **To emboss text**

1. Select the text you want to emboss.

2. From the Format menu, choose Font.

   The Font dialog box appears.

3. In the Effects box, select Emboss.

4. Choose OK.

Tip Embossing works best on a medium-toned background. If you emboss text on a dark or light background, the text is harder to read.

Superscripting and subscripting text

You can select text and raise it (superscript) or lower it (subscript) in relation to the text's baseline. The font size is automatically reduced.

▶ **To superscript and subscript text**

1. Select the text that you want to superscript or subscript.

2. From the Format menu, choose Font.

   The Font dialog box appears.

3. In the Effects box, select Superscript or Subscript.

4. In the Offset box, enter a percentage by which to offset the selected text.

   You can enter the percentage number by clicking the arrows or by typing a number.

5. Choose OK.

Replacing fonts

Sometimes you'll need to replace specific fonts in your presentation—when you move files between platforms, for example. When you replace a font with the Replace Fonts command, *all* the text using that font in your presentation changes.

▶ **To replace fonts**

1. From the Tools menu, choose Replace Fonts.

   The Replace Font dialog box appears.

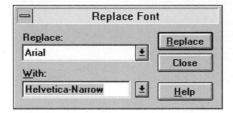

Click the down arrow to display more fonts.

If you selected text before choosing Replace Fonts, the font used in the selected text is highlighted. If no text is selected, the font currently listed on the Formatting toolbar appears in the Replace box.

You can scroll through the list in the Replace box to see all the fonts that are available to you.

2. Select the replacement font in the With box.

   You can scroll through all your system's available fonts to find one you like.

3. Choose Replace.

   The font is replaced by your new choice.

4. Choose Close.

Now all the text that was in the old font appears in the replacement font. Other text attributes (italics and so forth) aren't affected.

If you don't like the new font, choose Undo from the Edit menu before doing anything else.

Tip Be sure the font you choose is easily readable on the screen. You might need to increase the replacement font's size, too.

Hints for formatting text

- You can use more than one text style at a time. For instance, it can be **bold**, *bold and italic*, **bold and underlined**, or ***all three***. If you don't like the effect, you can always change the text back to plain.

- If you select text that contains a variety of attributes—some bold, some italic, and so on—the Font dialog box and the toolbar buttons will show no selections. If you choose one attribute for the entire selection, all other attributes will be overridden.

- Try using the Format Painter tool on the Standard toolbar to copy a text style you particularly like from one text object and apply it to another. Just select the text with the style you want to copy, and then click the Format Painter tool. Then select the object to which you want to apply the text style.

Formatting Paragraphs

There are certain formatting characteristics that apply to all the text in a paragraph. Line spacing, for example, affects all the lines in the paragraph. And alignment works the same way. When a formatting characteristic applies to a paragraph, you don't have to select the whole paragraph to apply it. Just click anywhere in the paragraph and proceed.

For in-depth procedures, in online Help see:

- Displaying the rulers
- Setting text indents
- Setting tabs

under "How to Format Paragraphs—In Depth" in the Chapter 4 Help Contents window.

How to Format Paragraphs

Changing a paragraph's alignment

PowerPoint gives you the option of aligning the text in paragraphs on the right, the left, or the center, or to justify the text. You can set paragraph alignment on the Slide Master, if you want, or you can set it for each individual object.

Here are some examples.

Aliquip ex ea commodo consequat Odio dignissim qui blandit praesent luptatum Vel illum dolore eu feugiat nulla delenit

Left alignment

Aliquip ex ea commodo consequat Odio dignissim qui blandit praesent luptatum Vel illum dolore eu feugiat nulla delenit

Center alignment

Aliquip ex ea commodo consequat Odio dignissim qui blandit praesent luptatum Vel illum dolore eu feugiat nulla delenit

Right alignment

Aliquip ex ea commodo consequat Odio dignissim qui blandit praesent luptatum Vel illum dolore eu feugiat nulla delenit

Justified text

▶ **To change a paragraph's alignment**

1. Select the paragraph or paragraphs you want to change.

   - To change the alignment of all paragraphs in a text object, select all the text.

   - To change the alignment of more than one paragraph, drag a selection that includes at least some text in the paragraphs to be changed.

   - To change the alignment of a single paragraph, click anywhere in the paragraph.

2. From the Format menu, choose Alignment.

   The Alignment cascading menu appears.

3. From the Alignment menu, choose the alignment you want.

Tip You can align the paragraph on the left or the center by clicking the left or center alignment tools on the Formatting toolbar.

Changing line or paragraph spacing

You use the Line Spacing command to adjust the space between lines of text and between paragraphs. You can decrease the spacing to make text fit better in a slide or increase the spacing to make text more readable.

▶ **To change line or paragraph spacing**

1. Select the paragraph or paragraphs in which you want to change either the line or paragraph spacing.

2. From the Format menu, choose Line Spacing.

    The Line Spacing dialog box appears.

3. Adjust the spacing by typing or by clicking the up or down arrow to change the value.

    - To change line spacing within the paragraphs, use the Line Spacing box.

    - To change spacing before or after a paragraph or paragraphs, use the Before Paragraph or After Paragraph box.

      You can adjust the spacing in lines or in points, using the drop-down list at the right of each adjustment box.

      Click Preview to see what effect the new line or paragraph spacing has on the text.

4. Choose OK.

Starting a new line within a paragraph

You can start a new line in a paragraph without creating a new paragraph. This is commonly called a "soft return." The new line will carry with it the attributes of the paragraph but will not have a separate bullet.

▶ **To start a new line in a paragraph**

- Press SHIFT+ENTER (Windows) or SHIFT+RETURN (Macintosh) and type the new line.

Adding and deleting bullets

PowerPoint automatically adds bullets to some text placeholders. Using the Bullet tool on the Formatting toolbar, you can delete the bullets if you want, or you can add bullets to other text. Or you can use the Bullet command on the Format menu to add custom bullets.

▶ **To add or delete bullets**

1. Select the bulleted items for which you want to add or delete the bullets.
2. Click the Bullet tool on the Formatting toolbar.

   The Bullet tool toggles bullets on and off.

Working with Text in Outline View

In Outline view, PowerPoint displays your presentation as an outline made up of the titles and main text from each slide. Each title appears on the left side of the window along with a slide icon and slide number. The main text is indented under the slide title. Graphic objects—pictures, charts, graphs, and so on—don't appear in Outline view except for a small notation on the slide icon.

Working in Outline view is particularly handy because you can see the text of your presentation as a whole, rather than just the text and pictures you see in Slide view. It's also easy to rearrange your points, move slides from one position to another, and apply formatting changes.

Here's what a presentation looks like when you're working on it in Outline view.

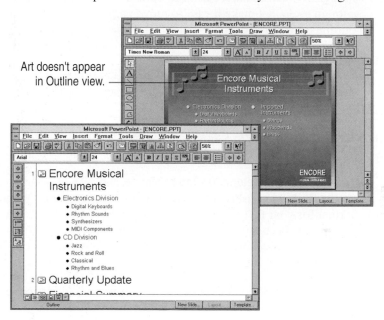

Art doesn't appear in Outline view.

Outline view contains only the titles and main text in your presentation.

Terms That Apply to Outlines

When you're working with outlines, you may find it helpful to understand these terms and ideas.

An outline has levels. There are different indentations at which paragraphs appear in an outline. Titles are always at the left and text is indented one to five levels to the right of a title.

An outline is made up of titles and text. When you look at an outline, you're looking at the titles and main text from your slides. Pictures and other visuals don't appear in an outline. Other text you've added using the Text tool (such as the date, for example) and embedded text and graphics won't show up either, since they're not part of the main text.

The Outlining toolbar When you switch to Outline view, the Outlining toolbar automatically appears.

Paragraphs can be moved as in an outline.   The Outlining and Formatting toolbars contain tools that make it easy to move paragraphs to different levels in the outline or to move them up and down within the outline. These functions are also available in Slide view and Notes view by using shortcut keys.

Slide icon   An icon appears next to each slide title in the outline. PowerPoint adds the icon to show you where each slide begins. A slide icon will tell you whether there are any graphics on the slide as well.

Outline Master   There's a master page where you add headers, footers, and so on to appear when you print the outline.

The Slide Master determines the outline format.   The format you select for the text on the Slide Master becomes the format for your outline. When you set up the format for your text on the Slide Master, you format levels for a list, set the amount of space to use for each indent, decide what kind of bullets to use for each level, and so on. Now, when you go to Outline view, you can see all your formatting from the Slide Master.

An outline can be printed.   Your outline appears in print according to the toolbar button settings that are applied at the time you print. For more on printing outlines, see Chapter 6, "Notes, Handouts, Slide Shows, and Printing."

Four-arrow pointer   This is the pointer you use to move paragraphs around on slides and in outlines.

How to Work with Text in Outline View

Typing an outline

▶ **To type an outline**

1. With a new presentation open, click the Outline View button on the status bar to go to Outline view.

   The number 1 and a slide icon appear in the left margin. The Outlining toolbar appears to the left of the window.

Outlining toolbar

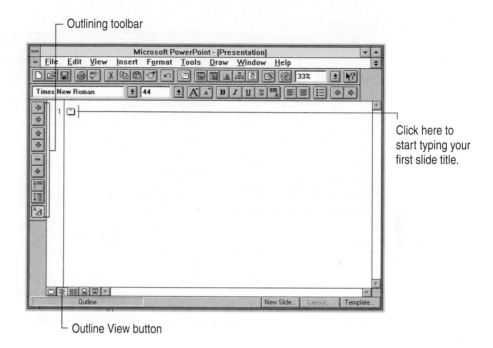

Click here to
start typing your
first slide title.

Outline View button

You type your presentation in Outline view and then add clip art, graphics, and other visuals in Slide view.

2. Type a title for the first slide, and press ENTER (Windows) or RETURN (Macintosh). Then click the Demote button on the Formatting toolbar.

    You are now working on the first bulleted level of the first slide.

3. Type a series of bullet items for the slide, pressing ENTER (Windows) or RETURN (Macintosh) at the end of each line.

Use the Promote tool to shift a selection up one level.

Use the Demote tool to shift a selection down one level.

Use the Move Up tool to move text forward in your presentation.

Use the Move Down tool to move text backward in your presentation.

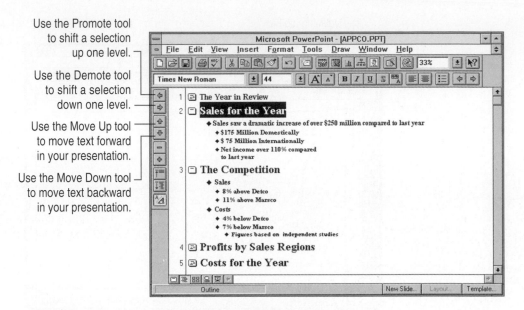

Press CTRL+ENTER (Windows) or OPTION+RETURN (Macintosh) to create a new slide in Outline view.

Use the Promote and Demote buttons to create various indent levels.

4. At the end of the last bullet point for a slide, press CTRL+ENTER (Windows) or OPTION+RETURN (Macintosh) to create the next slide.

5. Continue typing titles and text for the slides in your presentation.

    When you return to Slide view, you'll have a title and text for each slide you created.

Tip You can always click the Promote and Demote buttons to change levels in an outline at any time. If you want to promote or demote text in Slide View you can always use the Promote and Demote tools on the Formatting toolbar.

Selecting text in an outline

▶ **To select text in an outline**

- **To select the entire outline**—press CTRL+A (Windows) or COMMAND+A (Macintosh).

- **To select one slide**—click the slide icon or the slide number next to the title on the outline.

PowerPoint selects all the title and body text on the slide, plus any other objects that are on the slide but not visible in Outline view. (This way, if you move a slide, for example, all its objects are moved.)

- **To select a paragraph and all of its sublevels**—position the pointer to the left of the paragraph so the four-arrow pointer appears, and then click. Or triple-click anywhere in the paragraph.

- **To select a word**—double-click the word.

Working with text in an outline

Once you've created some slides—whether in Slide view or Outline view—you can edit your text in Outline view. Just as in Slide view, you can modify the style of the text by changing fonts, sizes, and styles. For example, you can italicize a word or make a phrase bold. However, if you want to change the text color or shadow style, you can only do that in Slide View.

▶ **To edit text in an outline**

1. Select the text.

2. Edit the text just as you would in Slide view.

   Most of the tools and menus for editing text in Slide view are also available in Outline view.

▶ **To format text in an outline**

1. Select the text you want to format.

2. Click the Bold, Italic, or Underline button on the Formatting toolbar.

   PowerPoint styles the selected text for you.

Moving slides in an outline

▶ **To rearrange your slides in outline form**

1. Click the slide icon of the slide you want to move.

2. Drag the icon up or down in the outline to reorder your slides.

   All the body text moves with the icon.

Promoting, demoting, and moving paragraphs in an outline

You can move a paragraph (or paragraphs) up or down a level in the hierarchy of the outline. When you promote a paragraph, it moves to the left; when you demote it, it moves to the right.

When you move a paragraph up, you exchange it with the one above; when you move a paragraph down, you exchange it with the one below.

▶ **To promote/demote a paragraph in an outline**

1. Click in the paragraph you want to promote or demote.

2. Click the Promote or Demote button on the Formatting toolbar.

   −or−

   You can position the pointer and then drag the paragraph left or right.

▶ **To move a paragraph up or down in an outline**

1. Click in the paragraph you want to move up or down.

2. Click the Move Up or Move Down button on the Outlining toolbar.

   −or−

   You can position the pointer and then drag the paragraph up or down in the outline.

Hints on making an outline

- Work with plain text to see more of your presentation at once. Click the Show Formatting button on the Outlining toolbar to view and print your presentation as plain text.

- You can display or hide text in your outline. Click the Show Titles button to display only titles for the entire presentation.

- When you print your outline, it prints in the same scale as the selected viewing scale

Using Text from Other Applications

In PowerPoint, you can import an existing outline to create a new presentation or add an outline to an existing presentation. You can import outlines from Microsoft Word or another word processor. PowerPoint can read outline files in RTF (rich text format) and plain text formats.

When reading a file from another presentation graphics program, such as Harvard Graphics® or Aldus Persuasion®, PowerPoint picks up the outline structure from the styles used in the file (a heading 1 becomes a title, a heading 2 becomes the first level of text, and so on). If the file contains no styles, PowerPoint uses the paragraph indents to create your outline. In plain text files, PowerPoint uses tabs at the beginning of paragraphs to define the outline structure.

If you're a Microsoft Word 6.0 user, you can use the PowerPoint feature called Report It. With Report It, you can export an outline from PowerPoint and launch Word with the press of a button. Then you can take advantage of the powerful word-processing capabilities of Word. Once you've edited your outline, you can use the Present It button in Word to bring the outline back into PowerPoint.

Note Imported outlines can have up to nine indent levels while PowerPoint outlines have six (one for titles and five for text). When you import an outline, all text that is level 6 and below is treated as level 5 text.

How to Use Outlines from Other Applications

Creating a presentation by importing or inserting an outline

PowerPoint creates slides for all first-level headings in an imported outline and adds the body text as indent levels. All text that is level 6 and below is treated as level 5 text. The format for the title and the text comes from the Slide Master in the current presentation.

▶ **To create a presentation by importing an outline**

1. From the PowerPoint File menu, choose Open.

   The Open dialog box appears.

2. Select Outlines in the List Files Of Type box.

   PowerPoint displays a list of file types that you can open as outlines in PowerPoint. RTF and plain text files are grouped under Outlines.

3. Find and select the file you want to use, and then choose the OK button.

   You can now customize the imported outline so that it reflects your ideas for the presentation.

▶ **To insert an outline into an existing presentation**

You can add slides to an existing presentation by inserting an outline, using the Slides From Outline command on the Insert menu. You do this in any view— Slide, Slide Sorter, Notes, or Outline.

1. Go to the slide after which you would like to add slides.

2. From the Insert menu, choose Slides From Outline.

3. Select the file to be used as an outline, and then choose OK.

   The slides appear after the current slide in your presentation.

   You can now tailor the content of the new slides to your presentation.

Exchanging outlines with Word using Report It

You can use the Report It feature to export an outline from PowerPoint and launch Word.

▶ **To exchange outlines with Microsoft Word 6.0 using Report It**

1. Open your presentation.

2. On the Standard toolbar, click the Report It button.

Report It button

Microsoft Word 6.0 is launched.

Your PowerPoint outline appears in a Word 6.0 document, where you can edit it using Word commands.

3. When you're finished working on your outline in Word 6.0, click the Present It button.

   Your edited outline appears in PowerPoint.

Tip   You can create an outline in Microsoft Word 6.0 and send it directly to PowerPoint using the Present It button.

How to Use a Table from Microsoft Word

Creating and inserting a table from Microsoft Word

In Microsoft Word, you can create tables in various formats. You can build a table in Word and then insert it into your presentation.

▶ **To create and insert a table from Microsoft Word**

1. Start Microsoft Word from PowerPoint by doing one of the following:

   - From the Insert menu, choose Microsoft Word Table.

   - Double-click an empty object placeholder on the current slide. When the Insert Object dialog box appears, select the Create New option button and select Microsoft Word Table from the Object Type list.

   - Choose the Table AutoLayout and double-click the Table placeholder.

   - Click the Insert Microsoft Word 6.0 Document button on the Standard toolbar.

2. Choose OK.

   The Word application menus and tools appear.

3. Use the Word tools and menus to create the table.

4. When you are finished, click anywhere on the slide to return to PowerPoint.

The table you have created is inserted in the current slide of your presentation. You can now move it, resize it, recolor it, add a shadow, add a frame, and crop it.

Editing a Microsoft Word table

▶ **To edit a Microsoft Word table**

   - Double-click the table.

     −or−

     Select the table, and, from the Edit menu, choose Edit Document Object.

     −or−

     The Microsoft Word tools and menus appear, and you can edit the table.

CHAPTER 5

Adding Visuals to Slides

PowerPoint is designed to help you produce professional-looking presentations quickly and efficiently without having to spend a lot of time on the artwork. PowerPoint helps you get your point across by giving you all sorts of ways to add strong graphic and visual support to your words.

This chapter describes how to work with all kinds of visuals—things you draw, AutoShapes you create using the toolbar, pictures you add from other applications, and clip art. You'll find out about making equations, inserting graphs and other visuals in your presentations, creating organizational charts, and adding special effects using Microsoft WordArt.

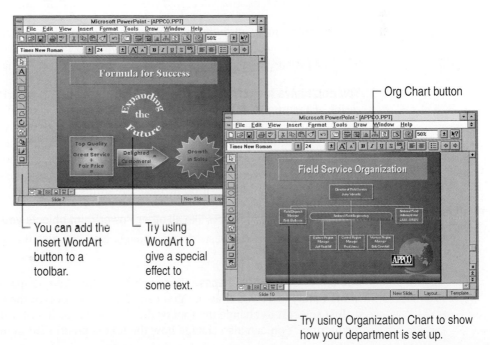

Org Chart button

You can add the Insert WordArt button to a toolbar.

Try using WordArt to give a special effect to some text.

Try using Organization Chart to show how your department is set up.

In This Chapter

Drawing Objects in PowerPoint

Here are some ideas that will help you understand more about drawing in PowerPoint.

Things you draw fall into two categories. One category includes lines, arcs, and freeforms. The other category includes rectangles, ellipses, and other shapes that we call AutoShapes. Each category has its own tools and attributes.

Drawn objects have attributes, just like other objects. For instance, they can have a border, a shadow, a color, and so on. The Drawing toolbars have buttons you can use as shortcuts for commands such as Line Style, Fill, and Shadow.

You don't have to draw an object perfectly the first time. PowerPoint has a whole series of features for resizing, altering, and adjusting objects after you've drawn them. You can change any attribute at any time. For instance, you can change an object's color, pattern, shadow, the color of its text, or even the shape of the object itself after you've drawn it. Because there are lots of ways you can position objects on slides, you don't have to draw objects in exactly the right position. You can move, align, and reposition them at any time.

You can treat drawn objects like all other PowerPoint objects you work with.
You can cut, copy, and paste drawn objects. You can also duplicate, delete, resize, move, and color them.

You can attach text to shapes. To attach text to an AutoShape, start typing immediately after you draw it. You can change the look of the text after you type it. Just select it to change the font or the size, italicize it, color it, and apply other formatting. You can also change how the text is positioned in the shape by changing the alignment and other paragraph attributes. You can't, however, attach text to arcs, freeforms, and lines.

Terms That Apply to Drawing

Some of the terms used to describe objects may be unfamiliar. Here are the terms you'll need to know.

Object   An object is a single component of your drawing. You draw objects with the text and drawing tools on the Drawing and AutoShapes toolbars. Objects can be rectangles, squares, circles, ovals, rectangles with rounded corners, diamonds, trapezoids, stars, freeforms, arcs, graphs, and so on.

Selection box   The selection box is the outline that appears around an object to indicate that it's selected. You'll also see the resize handles when an object is selected so you can work on it; you see an outline *without* handles when you're adding text to an object. You can move a selected object by dragging its border.

Resize handles   Resize handles are the squares that appear at each corner and on the edges of an object when you select it by clicking its border. Dragging a resize handle resizes the object.

Resize handle ¬

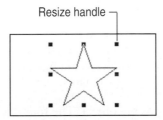 

You see resize handles when the object is selected. You see the object's border and a fuzzy selection box when you're adding text.

Adjustment handle   The adjustment handle is a diamond the size of a resize handle. It usually isn't on a corner. Depending on the shape of the object, you can adjust its features by dragging this handle. For example, you can adjust a rounded rectangle to be more rounded or less rounded.

Control handle   The control handle is the colored square that appears at each vertex of all arcs and freeforms when you are editing them. You use control handles to edit arcs and freeforms.

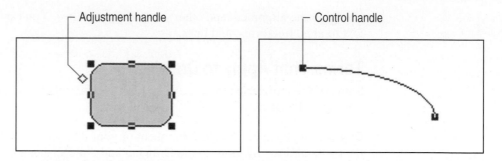

Use the adjustment handle to change the look of a rounded rectangle. Use a control handle to resize or edit an arc.

Attributes   Attributes are features of an object such as its line color, shadow, and fill color.

Shape   Shape is the form of an object. A rectangle is a shape, and so is a circle, a triangle, or a trapezoid. Shape is also an attribute. You can change an object's shape in one step without redrawing the object.

Regular shape   A regular shape is a perfectly proportioned shape that can be inscribed within a square. Circles and squares are regular shapes.

Constraint keys   When you draw shapes, you can hold down the SHIFT key as well as the CTRL key (Windows) or the OPTION key (Macintosh) to constrain how an object is drawn. Using these keys, you can draw an object from its center, or you can draw regular shapes, such as circles and squares.

Border   A border is the line that forms the object. The four lines of a rectangle are its border; the three lines of a triangle are its border; and the single curved line that forms a circle is its border. You change the border's style by changing the line style for the object.

Vertex/vertexes   A vertex is the point where two straight lines meet.

About the Drawing Toolbars

PowerPoint provides three Drawing toolbars with buttons that give you quick access to the commands you use most often when you draw. You can move any toolbar by clicking between buttons and then dragging, or by dragging the title bar.

The Drawing toolbar   The Drawing toolbar contains the tools you use to draw all sorts of objects such as lines, circles, and boxes. You'll also find tools here to alter the objects once you've drawn them—the Free Rotate tool, Line on/off, and the Fill on/off, for example.

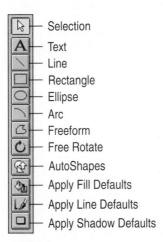

- Selection
- Text
- Line
- Rectangle
- Ellipse
- Arc
- Freeform
- Free Rotate
- AutoShapes
- Apply Fill Defaults
- Apply Line Defaults
- Apply Shadow Defaults

Drawing toolbar

The AutoShapes toolbar The tools on the AutoShapes toolbar are used for drawing commonly used shapes—stars, triangles, and diamonds, for example. You display the AutoShapes toolbar by clicking the AutoShapes button on the Drawing toolbar or by using the Toolbars command on the View menu.

Tip You can move your favorite AutoShape buttons to the Drawing toolbar. From the Tools menu, choose Customize, and then, under Categories, select AutoShapes. Drag the button or buttons to the Drawing toolbar.

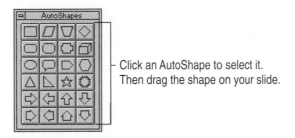

Click an AutoShape to select it.
Then drag the shape on your slide.

AutoShapes toolbar

The Drawing+ toolbar The Drawing+ toolbar is available when you choose the Toolbars command from the View menu. Here you'll find special tools to modify your visuals. You can use the Drawing+ toolbar to change fill color, for example, or to alter the width of a line.

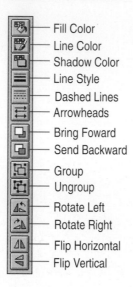

Fill Color
Line Color
Shadow Color
Line Style
Dashed Lines
Arrowheads
Bring Foward
Send Backward
Group
Ungroup
Rotate Left
Rotate Right
Flip Horizontal
Flip Vertical

Drawing+ toolbar

About the Drawing Tools

The drawing tools make it easy to draw typical presentation objects.

Here are some examples of the types of objects you can draw with the PowerPoint drawing tools.

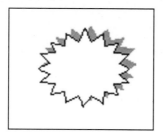 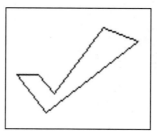 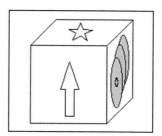

Drawing tools share attribute settings. Whether you draw a line or a rectangle, for example, the line style and color are the same for each object.

Drawing Rectangles, Ellipses, and Other AutoShapes

An AutoShape is a shape that you draw automatically when you select its icon and then drag. Tools for drawing AutoShapes appear in two places: on the Drawing toolbar and on the AutoShapes toolbar. The rectangle and the ellipse appear on the Drawing toolbar, while the rest of the automatic shapes (the star, arrows, and so forth) are on the AutoShapes toolbar.

You can also create "regular" shapes—a perfect square, circle, star, and so on—using the AutoShapes tools by holding down the SHIFT key as you drag to draw them.

Once you've created an AutoShape, you can change it to any other AutoShape. You can change a square into an ellipse, an ellipse into a cross, and so on, using the Change Shape command on the Draw menu. The new shape appears within the imaginary bounding box of the original shape.

A text object has an automatic shape—a rectangle. You can see it if you add a border to text you've typed. You can change that shape just as you can any other automatic shape.

Many AutoShapes have an adjustment handle; you drag the handle to alter the shape. Or you can resize the AutoShape by dragging one of its resize handles. In general, you can do anything to an AutoShape that you can do to any PowerPoint object—move it, resize it, change its color, and so forth.

For details about how to manipulate PowerPoint objects, see Chapter 3, "Working with PowerPoint Objects."

How to Draw AutoShapes

Drawing an AutoShape

You use the same basic technique to draw every kind of AutoShape. You click an AutoShape button on the Drawing or AutoShapes toolbar and then drag the shape on the slide.

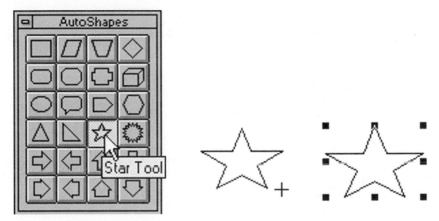

Click the button on the AutoShapes toolbar for the object you want to draw. Then drag the cross-hair pointer away from the point of origin to draw the object. Release the mouse when the object is the size you want. The object is automatically selected.

▶ **To draw an AutoShape**

1. Click the AutoShapes button on the Drawing toolbar to display the AutoShapes toolbar.

2. Click the tool for the shape you want on the AutoShapes toolbar.

   The pointer turns into a cross hair when you move it over the slide.

3. Click where you want the shape to begin, and then drag.

4. Release the mouse button where you want the shape to end.

   Just start typing to add text to the shape. Click the AutoShapes tool on the Drawing toolbar again to hide the AutoShapes toolbar.

Drawing a regular shape

▶ **To draw circles, squares, and other regular shapes**

Press the SHIFT key as you drag to draw squares, circles, and other regular shapes. (A regular shape is one that can be inscribed within a square.)

■ Click the tool for the shape you want and hold down the SHIFT key while drawing.

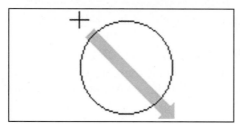

To draw a regular shape, hold down the SHIFT key as you drag the shape.

Tip You can turn a shape into a regular shape—say an ellipse into a circle, for example—by selecting the shape and then double-clicking a resize handle.

Drawing from the center outward

▶ **To draw a shape from the center outward**

- Click the tool for the shape you want to draw, and hold down the CTRL key (Windows) or the OPTION key (Macintosh) while drawing.

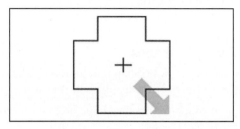

When you draw using the CTRL (Windows) or OPTION (Macintosh) key, the shape expands around its center point.

▶ **To draw regular objects from the center outward**

- Click the tool for the shape you want, hold down the SHIFT+CTRL keys (Windows) or the SHIFT+OPTION keys (Macintosh), and then drag.

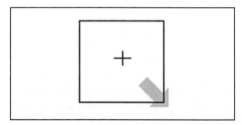

Use SHIFT+CTRL (Windows) or SHIFT+OPTION (Macintosh) to draw a regular shape from the center outward.

Tip A regular shape doesn't have to remain regular. If you drag its resize or adjustment handles, its size and proportions change accordingly.

Changing the shape of an AutoShape

Sometimes you'll want to change one AutoShape into another. For example, say you'd rather have a 3-D box than the rectangle you drew. In PowerPoint, it's easy to change an AutoShape into any other one that's available.

▶ **To change the shape of an AutoShape**

1. Select the object you want to change.
2. From the Draw menu, choose Change AutoShape.

3. Select another shape from the AutoShapes cascading menu.

   The new shape appears in place of the old shape.

Tip Try flipping and rotating shapes for more shape options. If text is attached to the shape, it rotates but will not flip

---

Hints for working with shapes

- When you change one AutoShape into another, the new shape keeps the characteristics of the old shape—its fill, line style, color, and so on.

- To add text to a shape, select the shape and begin typing. The text appears in the object.

- You can resize an object or a group of objects to an exact percentage by choosing Scale from the Draw menu.

- If you use the adjustment handle to adjust the shape of an object and then change it to another AutoShape (for instance, from a rounded rectangle to a cross), PowerPoint generally retains the adjustments you made. If the objects are too dissimilar, the adjustments aren't retained.

Drawing Lines, Arcs, and Freeforms

A freeform object can be anything: a closed polygon, a puffy cloud, an outline of a state, or even your name in cursive. Freeform objects can consist of straight lines, arcs, freehand lines, or a combination of the three. In fact, all freeform lines are straight lines. What appears to be a curved line is really just a series of very short straight lines connected to one another. This becomes obvious when you edit freeform objects.

Freeform objects can be closed or open. A closed freeform has the end of its last line connected to the beginning of its first line. An open freeform doesn't have its first and last lines connected. There are slightly different procedures for drawing closed and open freeform objects.

You draw lines and arcs using the corresponding tools on the Drawing toolbar. You draw open and closed polygons, freeforms, and combined polygons and freeforms using the Freeform tool on the Drawing toolbar.

Here are some examples.

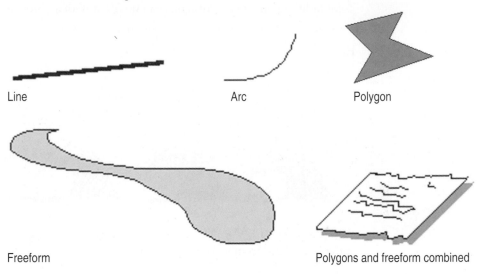

Line   Arc   Polygon

Freeform   Polygons and freeform combined

You can add attributes to lines, arcs, and freeforms. You can color lines, change their thickness, add arrowheads, or make them dotted or dashed. Lines can't be filled, however. Arcs and freeforms can be filled and colored, and their borders can be made thicker, dotted, or dashed. They can also have arrowheads.

Lines, arcs, freeforms, and pictures can't be converted into AutoShapes with the Change Shape command, and text cannot be attached to them except by grouping.

A polygon is defined as a series of points joined by lines.

Here are some examples.

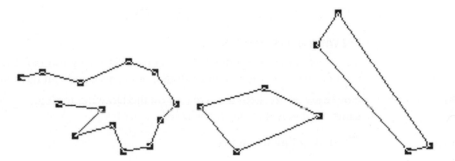

You can draw a closed polygon or an open one (where the last point and the first point aren't connected). Polygons can be filled with a color, just like other shapes.

You can use the Freeform tool to draw freehand shapes.

Here are some examples of what you can do.

You use two pointers for drawing freeform objects: a pencil for drawing freehand, and a cross-hair pointer for making polygons.

The pencil pointer and the cross-hair pointer

For in-depth procedures, in online help see:

- Changing the angle of an arc
- Editing a freeform object

under "How to Draw Lines, Arcs and Freeforms—In Depth" in the Chapter 5 Help Contents window.

How to Draw Lines, Arcs, and Freeforms

Drawing a line or an arc

You draw a line using the Line tool on the Drawing toolbar. Lines can be different thicknesses and colors, can be dotted or dashed, and can have arrowheads.

You draw an arc with the Arc tool on the Drawing toolbar. Arcs can have the same attributes that lines can have.

Line tool

Arc tool

▶ **To draw a line or an arc**

1. Click the Line or Arc tool to select it.

   The pointer turns into a cross-hair pointer when you move it over the slide.

2. Click where you want the line or arc to begin, and then drag.

3. Release the mouse button where you want your drawing to end.

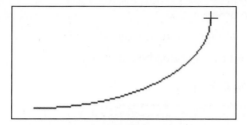

Click where you want the arc to end.

You can draw a regular arc using the constraint keys:

- SHIFT—Hold down the SHIFT key while drawing an arc to draw a quarter of a circle.

- CTRL/OPTION—Hold down the CTRL key (Windows) or the OPTION key (Macintosh) while drawing an arc to center it on the starting point of the pointer.

- SHIFT+CTRL/OPTION—Hold down the SHIFT+CTRL keys (Windows) or the SHIFT+OPTION keys (Macintosh) to draw a quarter of a circle centered on the starting point of the pointer.

Changing the style of a line

You can change the thickness of lines or change them into dashed or dotted lines. You can even add arrowheads if you want.

▶ **To change the style of the line or arc**

1. Select the line or arc.

2. From the Format menu, choose Colors And Lines.

   The Colors And Lines dialog box appears.

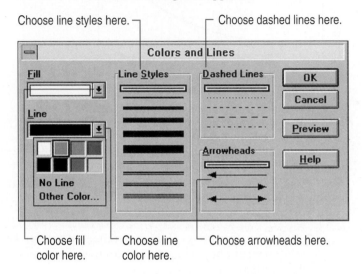

Choose line styles here. ⌐   ⌐ Choose dashed lines here.

Choose fill color here.   Choose line color here.   Choose arrowheads here.

3. Choose the styles you want under Line Styles, Dashed Lines, or Arrowheads, and then choose OK.

Rotating a line or an arc

When you rotate a line, you use the constraint keys or the Rotate tool; when you rotate an arc, you use the Rotate tool on the Drawing toolbar.

▶ **To rotate a line from its center point**

1. Select the line.

2. Click the Rotate tool on the Drawing toolbar.

3. Drag a handle to rotate the line.

   Be sure to release the mouse button before releasing the CTRL key (Windows) or OPTION key (Macintosh). Otherwise, the line won't stay rotated.

▶ **To rotate an arc from its center point**

1. Select the arc.

2. Click the Rotate tool on the Drawing toolbar.

3. Drag a handle to rotate the arc.

Filling an arc or a freeform

▶ **To fill an arc or freeform**

1. Select the arc or freeform.

2. From the Format menu, choose Colors And Lines.

   The Colors And Lines dialog box appears.

3. Select a color in the Fill box, and choose OK.

Resizing an arc

▶ **To resize an arc**

You can shorten or lengthen an arc without changing its position.

1. Double-click the arc to select it.

   When you see handles at each end of the arc, it's selected.

2. Drag one end of the arc to make the arc shorter or longer.

   When you first draw an arc, it is one quarter of an ellipse. You can extend the arc to create a pie wedge or rainbow shape by dragging a resize handle. Dragging a resize handle also lets you change the angle of the arc.

Drawing a polygon

Freeform tool

You use the Freeform tool to draw a polygon. Basically, you click wherever you want a point of the polygon to appear in the drawing. You can create closed or open polygons.

▶ **To draw a polygon**

1. Click the Freeform tool on the Drawing toolbar.

   The pointer turns into a cross-hair pointer when you move it over the slide.

2. Click where you want to position the first vertex of the polygon.

   Don't hold the mouse button down while you draw.

3. Click where you want the next point to appear.

4. Click until you have the shape you want.

5. To finish a closed polygon, click next to the first vertex.

−or−

To create an open polygon, double-click the end of the last line, or click once and press ESC or ENTER (Windows) or RETURN (Macintosh).

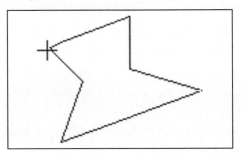

To create a closed polygon, click next to the first vertex.

Changing the shape of a polygon

You move, delete, or add vertexes to change the shape of a polygon.

▶ **To change the shape of a polygon**

1. Double-click the polygon.

   Handles appear on each vertex.

2. Drag any of the vertexes to change the polygon's shape.

   −or−

   Use CTRL+click (Windows) or OPTION+click (Macintosh) to add or delete a vertex.

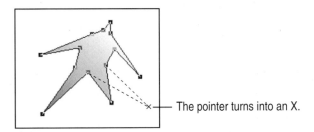

The pointer turns into an X.

Drag a vertex to reshape a polygon.

Drawing freehand

▶ **To draw freehand**

1. Click the Freeform tool on the Drawing toolbar.

   The pointer turns into a cross-hair pointer when you move it over the slide.

2. Place the cross-hair pointer where you want to begin drawing.

3. Hold down the mouse button.

   The drawing pencil appears.

4. Move the mouse to draw shapes on the screen. As long as you keep the mouse button down, you have access to the pencil.

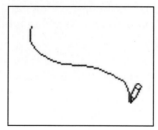

5. To create a closed drawing, put the pencil near the beginning of the starting point, release the mouse button, and click.

   –or–

   To create an open drawing, double-click the end of the drawing, or click once, release the mouse, and press ESC or ENTER (Windows) or RETURN (Macintosh).

Tip You can combine polygons and freehand drawings in a single freeform.

Hints for drawing freeforms

- Try increasing the view size to 200 percent or 400 percent for more detailed drawing.

- When drawing with the Freeform tool, try setting your mouse to the slowest tracking speed to get smoother curves and more precise control as you draw. Mouse speed is set in your computer's control panel.

- To constrain a line or a side of a polygon to vertical, horizontal, or 45 degrees, press SHIFT as you draw.

- Open freeforms and arcs are always drawn unfilled. If you want, say, a filled arc (a pie wedge), select the arc and choose a fill color in the Colors And Lines dialog box on the Format menu. You can also click the Apply Fill Attributes button on the Drawing toolbar to fill the object with the current fill color.

- Dotted and dashed lines are available for any freeform or arc. Arrows, though, can only be attached to unfilled arcs and unfilled, open freeforms.

- To remove the last vertex from a figure before you complete it, make sure the mouse button is released and then press BACKSPACE (Windows) or DELETE (Macintosh). Continue pressing BACKSPACE or DELETE to remove consecutive vertexes.

- To draw a combination figure (with straight edges and freehand sections in the same figure), alternate between clicking and dragging.

- You can scale a multiple selection by grouping several objects and then using the Scale command on the Draw menu.

- When you scale a multiple selection, each object scales around its own center. To scale around a common center, choose Group from the Draw menu, then scale the objects, and then choose Ungroup from the Draw menu.

Working with Imported Visuals

PowerPoint objects aren't limited to those you draw yourself. You can import clip art, pictures, movies—almost any computer image—into PowerPoint. This feature allows you to take advantage of the libraries of artwork already available without having to draw new artwork yourself.

PowerPoint can import images from other applications. These images can then be edited within PowerPoint; they can be moved and resized, and some can be recolored. You can also ungroup some pictures into their component objects so you can work with them. When you ungroup a picture, you disassemble it into

PowerPoint objects that, when regrouped, become a PowerPoint group (not a picture).

Adding Clip Art to Your Slides

If you've installed the PowerPoint ClipArt Gallery, you'll find it easy to dress up your presentations with the collection of professionally designed images. You have access to more than 1,000 pieces of clip art—everything from maps to people, and from buildings to scenic backgrounds.

You can also add your own images to the ClipArt Gallery, so they're readily accessible when you're working in PowerPoint. The ClipArt Gallery also includes a Find feature that helps you locate just the right images for your presentation.

You can change the size, location, and appearance of clip art once it's on a slide. You can easily replace one clip art image with another or edit a clip art image on your slide. You can also convert the image to groups of PowerPoint objects and work with those logical groups/objects just like any other drawn objects.

The ClipArt Gallery has its own Help system. If you need help, just choose the Help button in the ClipArt Gallery. You'll find useful information on adding your own pictures to the ClipArt Gallery and keeping the Gallery up-to-date, as well as suggestions on how you can personalize the ClipArt Gallery to suit your own needs.

How to Add Clip Art to Your Slides

Adding clip art

There are several ways to open the ClipArt Gallery so you can find and copy the image you want. Use the method that seems easiest for you.

▶   **To add clip art to your slides**

1. Click the Insert Clip Art button on the Standard toolbar.

    −or−

    Double-click a clip art placeholder on an AutoLayout.

    −or−

    From the Insert menu, choose Clip Art.

    The ClipArt Gallery opens.

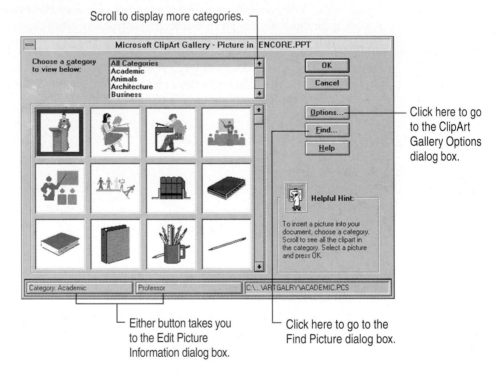

Scroll to display more categories.

Click here to go to the ClipArt Gallery Options dialog box.

Either button takes you to the Edit Picture Information dialog box.

Click here to go to the Find Picture dialog box.

2. Select the image you want by double-clicking it or by selecting it and choosing OK.

    The image appears on your slide.

> **Note** The first time you open ClipArt Gallery, you'll be asked if you want to add clip art from PowerPoint. Once you add PowerPoint clip art, you won't be asked again.

Replacing a clip art image in your presentation

▶ **To replace a clip art image**

- Double-click the image on your slide to open the ClipArt Gallery. You can then select another image from the ClipArt Gallery.

  You can't access the ClipArt Gallery in this way if you've ungrouped the image and changed it into a PowerPoint object.

Ungrouping clip art so you can modify it

If you want to work with a clip art image to modify it, you can ungroup it so that the image becomes groups of PowerPoint objects.

▶ **To ungroup clip art to modify it**

1. Select the clip art image on your slide.
2. From the Draw menu, choose Ungroup.

Now you can work with the groups and objects that make up the image. When you're done, you may want to regroup the art so you can move and resize it as one object.

> **Tip** You can create interesting effects by ungrouping clip art images into their individual elements, and then moving, duplicating, and recoloring them. You can even try combining elements of different clip art images.

Finding a piece of clip art

▶ **To find a particular piece of clip art**

1. Open the ClipArt Gallery by clicking the Insert Clip Art tool on the Standard toolbar, double-clicking a clip art placeholder on an AutoLayout, or by choosing Clip Art from the Insert menu.

2. In the ClipArt Gallery, choose Find.

The Find Picture dialog box appears.

Here are your options
for search criteria.

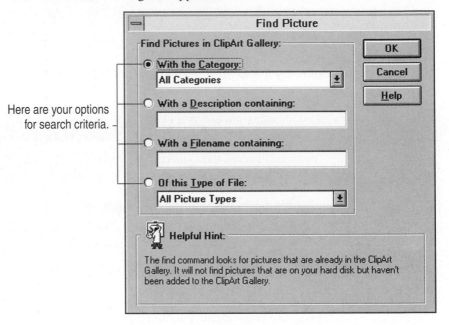

3. Depending on what picture you're looking for, you have a number of choices
    in the Find Pictures In ClipArt Gallery box.

-   **With the Category**—Select this option to search by category, both those
    included in the Microsoft ClipArt Gallery and any categories you've
    created.

-   **With a Description containing**—Select this option to search with
    keywords, such as "flower," "airplane," or "mountain." Note that choosing
    a word such as "flower" won't necessarily result in finding all the pictures
    of flowers in the ClipArt Gallery. Those with names such as "daisies"
    won't be found.

-   **With a Filename containing**—Select this option to search for a file by
    typing in any portion of the picture filename.

-   **Of this Type of file**—Select this option to look for pictures you've added
    to the ClipArt Gallery that are of a different type than those contained in
    Microsoft's clip art. This selection allows you to look for only bitmaps,
    TIFFs, metafiles, and so on.

Adding art to the ClipArt Gallery

▶ **To add art to the ClipArt Gallery**

1. Open the ClipArt Gallery by clicking the Insert Clip Art tool on the Standard toolbar, double-clicking a clip art placeholder on an AutoLayout, or by choosing Clip Art from the Insert menu.

2. In the ClipArt Gallery, choose Options.

   The Options dialog box appears.

3. In the Options dialog box, choose Add.

   The Add Clipart dialog box appears.

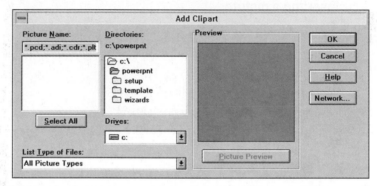

4. Go to the appropriate file, and select the picture you want to add. If necessary, select the type of picture in the List Type Of Files box.

5. You can choose the Picture Preview button if you want to see a thumbnail version of the picture.

6. Choose OK.

   The Add Clipart dialog box changes and asks you which category you want to place your picture in. You can also add a short description, if you want.

7. When you're finished, choose Add.

   If you change your mind, you can choose Don't Add.

Inserting Pictures on Your Slides

You'll find it easy to personalize your presentations by using the PowerPoint Insert Picture command to add all kinds of pictures—scanned photographs and line art, photos and artwork from CDs, and so on. Artwork might include your company's logo, even a piece of custom-designed art. Any picture, whether it's black-and-white or color, can be inserted into your presentation.

PowerPoint recognizes a number of different picture formats. You need to make sure you save your picture in an appropriate format before trying to insert it into a presentation. If you save it as a TIFF (tagged-image file format) file, for example, PowerPoint will recognize it when you want to add it to your presentation.

Tip You can check the kinds of file formats available by checking what's listed in the List Files Of Type box when you choose Picture from the Insert menu. If you didn't install all graphic filters available when you installed PowerPoint and you want to add more file formats, you can rerun Setup.

How to Insert Pictures on Your Slides

Inserting a picture

▶ **To insert pictures into a PowerPoint presentation**

1. Open your PowerPoint presentation and go to the slide to which you want to add a picture.

2. From the Insert menu, choose Picture.

    The Insert Picture dialog box appears.

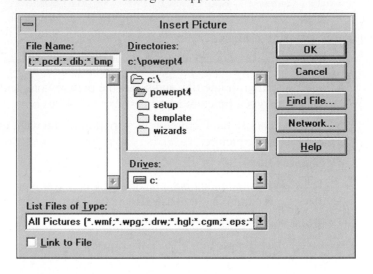

Notice that you don't have to specify which format your artwork is in. The default includes all the formats that PowerPoint recognizes and that are installed.

3. Go to the directory (Windows) or folder (Macintosh) in which you've stored your artwork.

4. Select the file, and then choose OK.

    The picture appears on the slide. (You may see a dialog box before the picture appears.) You can now move it, resize it, add a border, and so on.

Working with Embedded Visuals

With so many applications available, it makes sense to use information from other applications in your presentations. PowerPoint comes with several supplementary applications that let you take advantage of *object linking and embedding*, or OLE. When you *embed* an object, say a chart from Microsoft Graph, you make use of a supplementary application and its specialized tools. At other times, you might use an application such as Microsoft Excel to embed a spreadsheet. In PowerPoint, you can embed objects such as:

- Graphs (from Microsoft Graph)
- Organizational charts (from Microsoft Organization Chart)
- WordArt (from Microsoft WordArt)
- Excel charts (from Microsoft Excel)
- Equations (from Equation Editor)

There are also many other OLE applications you can use to produce specialized visuals for your PowerPoint presentation.

The supplementary applications included with PowerPoint come with their own Help systems. You can get specialized help while working with them by using their Help menus.

For more information about linking and embedding, see Chapter 7, "Using PowerPoint with Other Applications."

Creating Graphs

PowerPoint comes with a powerful supplementary application called Graph. You can create all kinds of graphs for your presentations without ever leaving PowerPoint by entering your data on the Graph data sheet. And you can edit a graph right on your PowerPoint slide.

This section introduces you to Graph by explaining how to add a graph to a slide. For detailed online information about using the full capabilities of Graph, press the F1 key (Windows) or the HELP key (Macintosh) while Graph is open.

For in-depth procedures, in PowerPoint Help see:

- Recoloring a graph

under "How to Create Graphs—In Depth" in the Chapter 5 Help Contents window.

How to Create Graphs

Inserting a graph

There are several ways to insert a graph into your presentation. You can choose an AutoLayout that already includes a graph placeholder, you can use the Insert Graph button on the Standard toolbar, or you can insert a graph on any slide layout by choosing Microsoft Graph from the Insert menu.

▶ **To insert a graph on an AutoLayout**

1. From the Insert menu, choose New Slide, and then pick an AutoLayout that includes a graph placeholder.

   −or−

   Click the Insert Chart button on the Standard toolbar.

   −or−

   From the Insert menu, choose Microsoft Graph.

   −or−

   From the Insert Object dialog box, choose Microsoft Graph 5.0.

   The Graph sample data sheet and graph appear, giving you access to all of the Microsoft Graph commands.

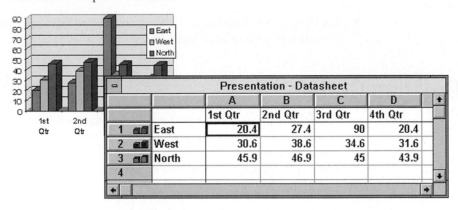

2. Start working on your graph.

   - To enter your data, click the data sheet window. Then type your data. You add information to a data sheet just as you would to a Microsoft Excel worksheet or a Microsoft Word table.

   - You can change the type of graph by selecting another one using the AutoFormat command on the Format menu.

3. When you finish, just click on the slide outside the graph to return to PowerPoint.

The graph you created is inserted in the current slide of your presentation. You can now move it, resize it, recolor it, add a shadow, add a border, and crop it.

Note If the Insert Object dialog box lists more than one version of Graph, it means you have different versions of the software available to you. All the available versions appear on the menu. You can use earlier versions to work on graphs you've already created. Or you can update your graphs using the latest version of Graph.

Editing a graph

You can edit your graph without leaving PowerPoint.

▶ **To edit a graph**

- Double-click the graph to start editing.

  The Graph menus and toolbars appear in your PowerPoint window. Now all you need to do is select the tools and choose the commands you want to use to update your graph.

Creating Organizational Charts

You don't need to create an organizational chart from scratch—PowerPoint provides a supplementary application called Microsoft Organization Chart that greatly simplifies the process for you.

Organization Chart has its own Help information that explains in detail how to create and edit organizational charts. To use that Help system, just press F1 (Windows) or HELP (Macintosh) while Organization Chart is open.

How to Create Organizational Charts

Creating an organizational chart

▶ **To insert an organizational chart**

- To start Organization Chart, do one of the following:

  From the Insert menu, choose Object, and then choose Microsoft Organization Chart.

  –or–

  Click the Insert Org Chart button on the Standard toolbar.

  –or–

Insert Org Chart button

Pick a slide layout that has a placeholder for a chart, using the Layout button. When the slide is on your screen, double-click the organization chart placeholder.

The Organization Chart window appears, displays a sample chart, and gives you access to all of its functions. Now you're ready to proceed.

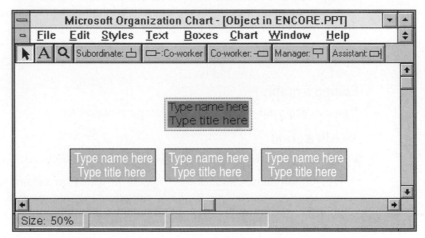

Click inside a box to add a name and position. To add more boxes, click one of the chart option buttons on the toolbar. Use the Organization Chart menus to change box colors, border color, and so on. You can change the type of chart by selecting another one from the Styles menu.

Editing an organizational chart

▶ **To edit an organizational chart**

- Double-click the chart on your slide.

   The Organization Chart tools and menus appear, and you can begin editing.

Creating Special Text Effects Using WordArt

Microsoft WordArt, available through the Insert WordArt button (which you can add to a toolbar by dragging it from the Customize Toolbars dialog box) and through the Object command on the Insert menu, lets you add special effects to text in your presentations. You can fit text into a variety of shapes, create unusual alignments, add 3-D effects, and so on using any TrueType® font installed on your system. You can use WordArt without leaving PowerPoint.

Refer to the Help system for WordArt to find out about its many features and functions by pressing F1 (Windows) or HELP (Macintosh) while WordArt is open.

How to Create Special Text Effects Using WordArt

Creating and inserting WordArt

▶ **To create and insert WordArt**

1. From the Insert menu, choose Object, and then choose the latest version of Microsoft WordArt.

   −or−

   Double-click an object placeholder.

   When the Insert Object dialog box appears, select the Create New button, and then choose Microsoft WordArt 2.0 from the Object Type list.

   The WordArt text entry dialog box and menus appear.

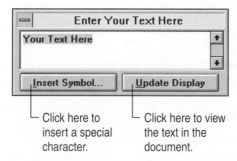

   Click here to insert a special character.   Click here to view the text in the document.

2. In the text entry box, type the text you want to format.
3. Click Update Display to view the text in the document.
4. Choose the text effect options you want from the WordArt menu and toolbar.

5. When you're finished creating the text effect, click in the PowerPoint window.

   The text effect you created is inserted in the current slide of your presentation where you can move it, resize it, recolor it, add a shadow, add a border, and crop it.

Inserting Equations

Equation Editor is a supplementary application that's shared among Microsoft applications. Using Equation Editor, you can create Greek symbols, integrals, various forms of fractions, subscripts and superscripts, and lots more. As in Graph, you can edit your equation in place without leaving PowerPoint.

Refer to the Help system for Equation Editor to find out about the many features and functions available to you as you work with equations by pressing F1 (Windows) or HELP (Macintosh) while Equation Editor is open.

How to Insert Equations

Inserting an equation on a slide

▶ **To insert an equation**

1. Add or display the slide to which you want to add the equation.
2. From the Insert menu, choose Object, and then select Microsoft Equation Editor 2.0 in the Object Type box.

   –or–

   Double-click an object placeholder.

   –or–

   If you've added the Insert Equation button from the Customize Toolbars dialog box to a toolbar, click the button.

   The Equation Editor window appears, giving you access to all of its menus and commands.

Insert Equation button

Editing an equation

You can edit an equation without leaving PowerPoint.

▶ **To edit an equation**

- Double-click the equation to start editing.

   The menus and toolbars available to you in Equation Editor appear in your PowerPoint window. Now all you need to do is choose the tools and commands you want to use to update your equation.

CHAPTER 6

Notes, Handouts, Slide Shows, and Printing

Speaker's notes and audience handouts are two useful components of a PowerPoint presentation. Once you've typed the text for your slides and added the art you want, you're ready to go to Notes view and type your own notes to use as a guide during your talk. If you want to provide your audience with copies of your slides, you can print audience handouts.

Electronic slide shows are another facet of a PowerPoint presentation. You don't have to have slides produced—you can give a show right on your computer. Slides fill the screen and use all the features you've incorporated—slide timing, for instance, or slide transitions and build slides. You can have hidden slides available in your presentation, or you can set up an option to branch to slides in another presentation. You can also use the rehearsal feature to have PowerPoint time your slides. The PowerPoint Viewer is available so you can share your presentations with others—just send them a copy of the PowerPoint Viewer disk, including the Viewer installation program, along with a copy of your presentation.

Printing is, of course, a direct way to see what you've created. You have lots of options: you can print one, two, three, or six slides per page; you can print color or black-and-white overheads; and you can print your notes or audience handouts.

In This Chapter

Creating and Using Notes and Handouts

Each slide in a presentation has an accompanying notes page, which includes a smaller version of the slide along with room for notes you type. You can print your notes and then use them to remember key points and asides during your presentation. You can make notes pages for as many slides as you want or type your script on notes pages to accompany your presentation. If you want to provide pages on which your audience can make notes, then print notes pages but leave the notes area blank.

You can also print handout pages for your audience so they can follow along as you make your presentation. Handout pages can contain two, three, or six slides per page. Handouts let your viewers "take the show with them" after the presentation is over. If you want, leave space on handouts so the audience members can take notes. Or add some text of your own.

For more information on printing, see "Printing a Presentation" later in this chapter.

You can add art to handout pages. Try putting a border around the slides, or place your company's logo on each handout page.

Both the notes pages and the handout pages have masters. You work with them just as you work with the Slide Master. You can format each master to suit your needs. Every notes page or handout contains the information you put on its master. If you want to add the date or page number to your notes or handouts, you do so on the masters. You can add visuals to the masters, such as logos or pieces of art, and you can add text, such as the name of the event at which you're presenting. If you want to reposition the slide image on all of your notes pages, change it on the Notes Master.

How to Create Notes and Handouts

Creating notes pages

Creating notes pages involves typing your notes as well as designing the look of the notes pages, using the Notes Master. You can always add design elements to an individual notes page if you want.

▶ **To create a notes page**

1. From the View menu, choose Notes Pages.

    The notes page that corresponds to the slide you're working on appears.

An image of the current slide appears at the top of the notes page. You type your notes in the box below the slide image.

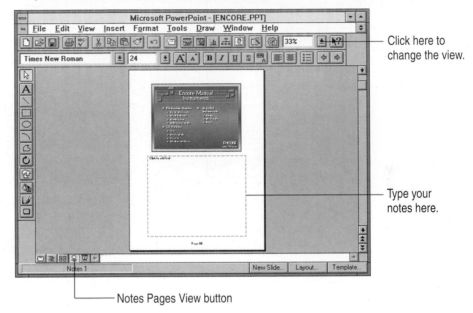

Click here to change the view.

Type your notes here.

Notes Pages View button

Move or resize the slide image if you need to make more room for your notes. You can also add a border around it to set it apart from your text.

2. Select the notes box by clicking inside the box, and then begin typing your notes.

   Click the Zoom Control button on the Standard toolbar if you want to enlarge the view.

Designing the look of the notes pages

Just as you design the look of your presentation using the Slide Master, you use the Notes Master to create a consistent look for every notes page.

▶ **To design the look of your notes pages**

1. From the View menu, choose Master, and then choose Notes Master from the Master cascading menu.

   The slide image appears at the top of the page, and the notes box is at the bottom.

2. Resize or change the location of the slide and the notes box to suit your needs.

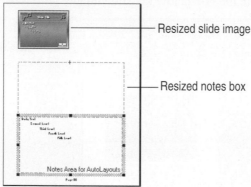

Resized slide image

Resized notes box

After you resize and move the slide image, you can select the notes box and drag a resize handle to increase the space for your notes.

3. Add art and text, if you want, or include the date, time, or page number.

You add art and text just as you do on the Slide Master—draw, add visuals, and so on. The same is true for adding the date, time, and page number, which you add using the commands on the Insert menu.

Creating audience handouts

You'll use the Handout Master to add art and text to your handouts. You see outlined boxes indicating where two, three, or six slides will be printed. To have your art and text appear on every handout, place it outside the outlined boxes on the Handout Master.

▶ **To add text to your handouts**

1. From the View menu, choose Master, and then choose Handout Master from the Master cascading menu.

The Handout Master appears.

If you print three slides per page,
they appear here on your handouts.

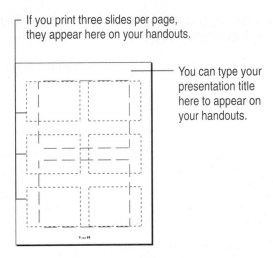

You can type your
presentation title
here to appear on
your handouts.

Type outside the outlined boxes to have your text appear on every page. You can add the presentation title, for example.

2. Select the Text tool on the Drawing toolbar, click where you want to add text (outside the outlined boxes for the layout you're going to use), and then begin typing.

Now, when you print your handouts, they'll look like this.

Here's a handout page with three slides per page, and with a presentation title added. Audience members can take notes on the right side.

Remember that whatever text you type on the Handout Master outside the outlined slide image boxes will be reproduced on every handout.

Adding date, time, or page number to audience handouts

Add the date, time, and/or page number to your Handout Master to have the information appear on every page.

▶ **To add the date, time, or page number to your handouts**

Choose the Date, Time, or Page Number command from the Insert menu, and then drag the box that appears at the center containing the symbol so that it appears where you want it.

For more information about time, date, and slide numbers, see "Adding the time and date and numbering slides" in Chapter 2, "Creating Presentations and Slides."

Hints for creating and using notes and handouts

- Try putting lines on your notes page if you plan to make some notes by hand later or if you want to give your notes pages to your audience so they can write down ideas. Draw a line, and then use the Duplicate command on the Edit menu to duplicate it. Position the duplicate where you want the second line to appear. Continue to choose Duplicate until you have the number of lines you want.

- You can change the attributes of the slide image and notes box on notes pages. You can change the colors, the borders, the text format, and so on, just as you can on a slide.

- Here's a fast way to switch between PowerPoint views. You can quickly switch between Outline, Slide, Notes Pages, and Slide Sorter views by clicking the buttons in the bottom left of the document window.

- Holding down the SHIFT key while clicking the view buttons in the bottom left of the document window will take you to the corresponding master.

Creating and Running Slide Shows

You can display your presentation electronically as a slide show, using your computer. When you do, the slides, with their text, art, and graphics, take up the full screen. All the tools, menus, and other screen elements are hidden so as not to detract from your show. Your computer becomes the equivalent of a slide projector.

By giving electronic presentations on your computer, you can:

- Save the time and expense of creating slides.

- Use your computer's color capability.
- Use special effects, such as transitions and builds, to add variety.
- Change your presentation right down to the last second.
- Give a presentation in a partially lit room as opposed to a darkened room.
- Annotate your slides as you give the presentation.
- Practice giving your presentation and set automatic timings for your slides to match your rehearsal times.
- Play movies and sounds during a slide show.
- Give slide shows from a play list.
- Hide slides to use for backup if you need them.
- Embed information such as a spreadsheet on a slide and open the spreadsheet during the slide show.

You can run your show electronically without any preparation by using the PowerPoint default settings. You'll probably want to see your slides full size on the screen before adding transitions and working on the timing. You can see the effect each slide has, try different transitions, change the timing to suit your talk, and generally design your electronic presentation so that it gets your point across in a clear, professional manner.

When you're fine-tuning your presentation, you'll be working in Slide view and in Slide Sorter view. It's easiest to work in Slide Sorter view—in which you view your presentation in miniatures, or thumbnails—to set transitions and slide timings and to create build slides and hidden slides.

For in-depth procedures, in online Help see:

- Creating "drill-down" documents
- Playing movies, sounds, OLE objects, and slides from other presentations during a slide show
- Branching to other slides during a slide show
- Using a Windows play list
- Sending out the PowerPoint Viewer with your presentation

under "How to Create and Run Slide Shows—In Depth" in the Chapter 6 Help Contents window.

Terms That Apply to Slide Shows

PowerPoint has a number of terms and features you should be familiar with when you're working in Slide Show view.

Build slide   A slide that starts with the first major bullet point and shows more major bullet points as the presentation proceeds; also known as a progressive disclosure slide. You choose whether you want to dim previous points on the slide as new points appear and what effect you want to use for each new bullet point (for instance, bullet points can "fly in" from the left, right, top, or bottom).

Hidden slide   A slide that doesn't automatically display during a slide show. You decide which slide or slides you want to be "hidden" and whether you want them to appear during your show. That way you can tailor a show to several different audiences.

Slide branching (Windows)   A slide show within a slide show; it's another way to tailor your presentation to suit different audiences. With slide branching, you can go to a whole separate group of slides during a slide show with the click of a button. You can create as many branches as you want for a PowerPoint presentation.

Drill down (branching to another application to show embedded information)
To pursue a particular topic in depth during a slide show by playing an OLE object during a slide show. For example, you might branch to a Microsoft Word table to provide more detail on a topic.

Running the show   Having PowerPoint advance the slides automatically for you, or controlling the pace of the show yourself, using the mouse or the keyboard. Or you can mix automatically timed slides with slides that need a manual click to advance.

Continuous loop   Displaying an automatic slide show on the screen continuously until you stop it by pressing the ESC key (Windows) or COMMAND+. (period) (Macintosh). This option is especially useful for an unattended presentation at a point-of-purchase display or for an on-screen presentation at a convention or trade show.

Transitions   Moves one slide off the screen and brings the next one on. Fading in from black and dissolving from one slide to another are two examples of transitions. You have a choice of transitions for each slide, and you can vary the speed of each transition. You can see a sample of each transition in the Transition dialog box, accessible from the Tools menu.

Timing   The amount of time a slide stays on the screen. You set the timings. For instance, you usually want more complex slides to remain on the screen longer. Timing is useful for live presentations as well as unattended presentations. You can always override preset timing and advance a slide using the mouse or keyboard.

Keyboard control   Using the keyboard to activate special features. For example, you can blank the screen while you speak to the audience so that the slide display isn't distracting. You can show a pointer on the slide and use it to highlight the content as you speak. You can advance the slides by clicking the mouse or by pressing a keyboard key. For a list of the options, see Appendix C, "PowerPoint Keyboard Shortcuts." To display the slide show control keys on the screen, press F1 (Windows) or HELP (Macintosh) during a show.

PowerPoint Viewer icon

PowerPoint Viewer PowerPoint comes with a special application called the PowerPoint Viewer that is designed to give electronic slide shows. You can use it yourself or give a copy of it to others who are going to be running your slide shows but who don't have PowerPoint. It's designed to be easy to use. (You can distribute copies of the Viewer freely. No additional license is needed.)

The PowerPoint Viewer has its own icon. When you install the PowerPoint Viewer, the icon will automatically be created in the program group (Windows) or folder (Macintosh) you choose.

How to Create and Run Slide Shows

Running a slide show

You can watch your presentation without setting timings and transitions by using the PowerPoint default settings. In this case, you run the show manually, and each transition is a simple "cut." Another easy way to run a presentation is to use the Slide Show dialog box, accessible from the View menu, to set timings and choose which slides you want to see. You can even choose to run the show over and over in a continuous loop.

▶   **To run a slide show**

1. Open the presentation.

2. From the View menu, choose Slide Show.

   The Slide Show dialog box appears.

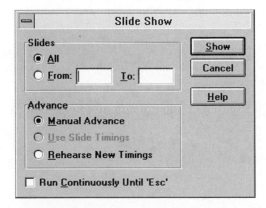

3. Under Slides, choose which slides you want to watch.

The default is All, which means that all the slides in your presentation will be in the slide show, beginning with the first slide.

If you want to see only certain slides, you can specify a range, for example, from slide number 4 through slide number 10.

4. Under Advance, choose how you want to advance the slides.

The default is Manual Advance. You'll need to click the mouse button to advance from slide to slide. (You can also use the arrow keys, the SPACEBAR, and the PAGE UP and PAGE DOWN keys.)

If you've set timings—how long each slide appears on the screen—you can select the Use Slide Timings option button, and the show will run automatically.

5. Choose Show.

The show begins.

Tip You can give a slide show beginning with the current slide. Just click the Slide Show button on the status bar.

Running a slide show in a continuous loop

▶ **To run a presentation in a continuous loop**

1. From the View menu, choose Slide Show.

The Slide Show dialog box appears.

2. Select the Run Continuously Until 'ESC' check box (Windows) or the Run Continuously Until COMMAND+. (period) check box (Macintosh).

Now, when you begin the presentation, it will run continuously until you cancel it.

Adding transitions to a slide show

Transitions are the visual special effects you see when you go from one slide to the next in an electronic slide show. You have lots of choices available. Here's how you set up transitions.

▶ **To add transitions to your slide show**

1. Click the Slide Sorter button on the lower left side of the document window.

2. From the Tools menu, choose Transition.

The Transition dialog box appears.

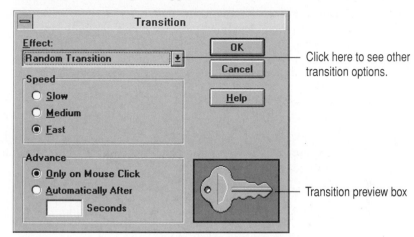

Click here to see other transition options.

Transition preview box

Every time you choose a transition, it's demonstrated in the preview box.

3. In the Effect box, select the transition you want.

    The transition you select is applied to the picture in the preview box. Click the picture to watch the transition again.

4. Choose how fast you want the transition to take place by selecting the Slow, Medium, or Fast option button.

    The speed is applied to the picture in the preview box.

5. Choose OK.

Transition icon

The transition is applied to the current slide. The transition icon is added below the slide in Slide Sorter view to show that you've set a transition for this slide.

You can also set slide transitions by changing to Slide Sorter view and then selecting an effect in the Transition Effects box on the Slide Sorter toolbar.

Tip   You can preview all of your transitions in Slide Sorter view by clicking the transition icon beneath each slide.

Setting slide timings

You can set separate timings, if you want, for all of the slides in your slide show. You can have the first slide appear for 10 seconds, the second slide for 15 seconds, the third for 8 seconds, and so on. There are two ways to set slide timings. You can type a number under Advance in the Transition dialog box (choose the Transition command from the Tools menu), or you can have PowerPoint set timings by using the Rehearse New Timings option in the Slide Show dialog box (choose the Slide Show command from the View menu).

▶ **To set slide timings manually**

1. Click the Slide Sorter button on the lower left side of the document window.

   Working in Slide Sorter lets you set the slide timings for all of your slides without changing views.

2. From the Tools menu, choose Transition.

   The Transition dialog box appears.

3. Under Advance, select the Automatically After [*blank*] Seconds option button.

   Select Automatically After [*blank*] Seconds to advance to the next slide after a preset time. Type the number of seconds that you want the slide to be on the screen before advancing to the next slide.

4. Choose OK.

   The slide timing is applied to the current slide.

▶ **To set slide timings while rehearsing**

You can adjust the timing for your slides during a slide show by choosing Slide Show from the View menu, and then selecting Rehearse New Timings. Cycle through the slides while you rehearse your presentation. PowerPoint keeps track of the length of time each slide is displayed and sets the timing accordingly.

1. From the View menu, choose Slide Show.

   The Slide Show dialog box appears.

2. Choose Rehearse New Timings under Advance, and then choose the Show button.

   When your slide show appears on the screen, you'll find a button in the lower left corner. The clock advances to show you how long the slide has appeared on-screen.

3. When you're ready to go to the next slide, click anywhere on the slide or on the clock.

   Repeat this process for the rest of your presentation.

4. When you're finished, choose Save if you're happy with your slide timings, or choose Cancel if you want to try again.

Creating build slides for a slide show

A build slide—also called a progressive disclosure slide—is one where each bullet point in the main text appears independently of the others. Use a build slide when you want to reveal bullet points one at a time. You set up the way you want each point to appear (to fly in from the left, for instance) and whether you want the other points already on the slide to dim when a new point is added.

Build button

▶ **To create a build slide**

1. From the Tools menu, choose Build.

   The Build dialog box appears.

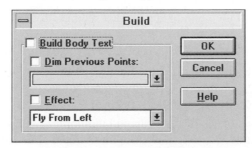

2. Decide how you want each bullet point to be displayed.

When you create a build slide, you can dim the previous points and use special effects to introduce each bullet.

- For a simple build, select the Build Body Text check box.

- If you want a point to dim and change color as the next point appears, select the Dim Previous Points check box. Then select a color on the drop-down Color menu.

- If you want the point to appear in a special way, select the visual effect you want in the Effect box.

There are lots of ways points can appear. As with the transitions, we suggest that you experiment and find the ones you like best.

Annotating slides during a presentation

While running a slide show, you can add temporary freehand annotations to your slides. For example, you might want to underline a point for emphasis as you are speaking. You don't have to worry about marking up your slides—any freehand annotations you make during a slide show are only temporary. The freehand annotation icon is a toggle: Click it once to turn it on, click it again to turn it off.

▶ **To annotate slides during a slide show**

1. Start your slide show.

2. Click the freehand annotation icon—the pencil—at the bottom right of the screen to turn the annotation feature on, and then move the mouse to make the pencil pointer appear.

Freehand annotation icon

3. Hold down the mouse button to write or draw on the screen during the slide show. Press the E key to erase annotations during a slide show. Otherwise, the annotation will disappear when you move to the next slide.

4. Click the freehand annotation icon again to turn the annotation feature off.

Using the PowerPoint Viewer

The PowerPoint Viewer is a separate application that comes with PowerPoint. You can use it to give slide shows on your computer, and you can give it to others so they can run your slide show on their computer. You can open the Viewer first and then pick the presentation you want to show, or you can set it up so that the Viewer opens a presentation automatically. If a presentation includes any branching to another presentation, that feature may be excluded when you use the Viewer.

Note People using the Viewer must have Microsoft Windows version 3.1 or later (Windows) or System 7.0 or later (Macintosh) installed on their computers.

**PowerPoint
Viewer icon**

▶ **To give a slide show using the PowerPoint Viewer**

1. Double-click the PowerPoint Viewer icon in the Program Manager (Windows) or on the Desktop (Macintosh).

   The PowerPoint Viewer dialog box appears.

2. Select the presentation you want to show, and then choose Show.

   The Viewer opens the presentation and the slide show begins.

Including hidden slides in a slide show

Hidden slides are slides that you can decide to exclude from a presentation. They are available to you if you want them. For instance, if you're presenting a budget overview, you might have hidden slides that show how you arrived at your figures. You might choose to show them, or you might not.

You can make a hidden slide in Slide view, Outline view, Notes view, or Slide Sorter view.

▶ **To create a hidden slide**

1. Display or select the slide you want to hide.

   If you're working in Slide Sorter or Outline view, you can select multiple slides.

2. From the Tools menu, choose Hide Slide.

   –or–

   If you're working in Slide Sorter view, click the Hide Slide button on the Slide Sorter toolbar.

   The slide is hidden during a slide show unless you choose to show it by clicking the icon in the lower right corner of the slide that precedes it.

Hide Slide button

In Slide Sorter view, the slide number is enclosed in a square with a line through it to signify that the slide is hidden.

⑤— This slide is hidden.

When a slide is hidden, the slide number is enclosed in a box with a line through it.

▶ **To display a hidden slide during a slide show**

On the slide that precedes a hidden slide in a slide show, you'll see the hidden slide icon in the corner of the screen when you move the mouse. You can skip the hidden slide by ignoring the icon, or you can display the slide.

Hidden slide icon

- Click the hidden slide icon.

  –or–

  Type **H**.

  –or–

  Type the slide number and press ENTER (Windows) or RETURN (Macintosh).

  The next slide displayed is the hidden slide.

Hints for creating and running slide shows

- Use the mouse arrow as a pointer while you speak.

- You can set the transitions and timings for all the slides at once by selecting all the slides in Slide Sorter view, using the Select All command on the Edit menu, and then choosing a transition. The transition you choose will be applied to all the slides in your presentation.

- Set the speed of your transitions to Fast. Transitions are meant to get you from one slide to the next. They should highlight your slides, not draw attention to themselves.

- Preview your presentation on the computer you'll be using for your slide show before delivering it before an audience. You'll be able to discover any "glitches" in advance.

- Don't dwell too long on one slide. While experimenting with slide timing, remember that viewers' attention will lag after a short amount of time. Two to three minutes per slide is a good pace. Consider breaking up slides with a lot of text into two or three slides with slightly different colors and graphic elements. You'll find it easier to keep your audience's attention with a faster pace.

- If you don't want your automatic presentation to be interrupted at trade shows or conventions, remove the keyboard and mouse once the show starts.

- For a smooth ending to your show, add a black slide as the last one in your presentation. That way, when your slide show finishes, you won't return to Slide view (which is what normally happens after the last slide). To create a black slide, add a blank AutoLayout to the end of your show and then choose the Slide Background command from the Format menu. Make sure the Display Objects On This Slide check box is *not* selected. Under Shade Styles, select None, and then change the color of the slide background to black by choosing the Change Color button and then choosing black in the Background Color dialog box.

Printing a Presentation

In PowerPoint, you can print your entire presentation—the slides, outline, speaker's notes, and audience handouts. You can print copies of your slides on paper or on overhead transparencies. Or you can create slides using a desktop film recorder or create a file to ship or modem to a service bureau that can then create slides.

No matter what you're printing, the process is basically the same.

Generally, the process you follow begins with opening the presentation you're printing. Then you identify the range of slides to be printed and the number of copies.

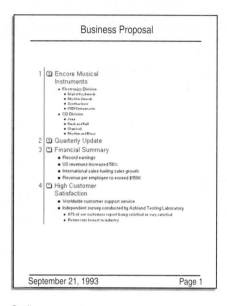

Outline

Audience handout

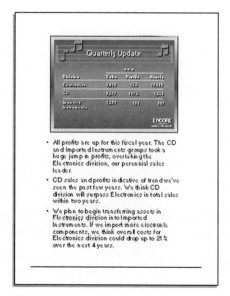

Notes page

Printed overhead

For in-depth procedures, in online Help see:

- Preparing files for a service bureau
- Getting professional color output from Genigraphics

under "How to Print Your Presentation—In Depth" in the Chapter 6 Help Contents window.

How to Print a Presentation

Setting up the slide format for printing

You should set up your slide format before you start your presentation by using the Slide Setup command on the File menu. The slide orientation you choose in the Slide Setup dialog box—landscape or portrait—determines the size of your printed slides. This task will ensure that what you see on the screen is what you'll see on the printed page and on your slides.

Normally, in PowerPoint, you won't need to change the printer setup information. But if you do, the dialog box you see is the same one you'd see if you were setting up the printer using either the Windows Control Panel or the Macintosh Chooser.

▶ **To set up the slide format**

PowerPoint is set up to create and print slides in landscape orientation that are 10 inches wide by 7.5 inches tall. Other options are available to you in the Slide Setup dialog box, accessible from the File menu.

1. From the File menu, choose Slide Setup.

   The Slide Setup dialog box appears.

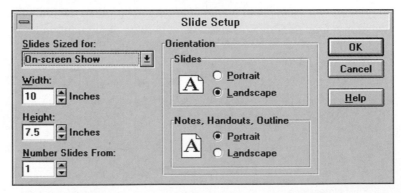

2. Choose the size you want in the Slides Sized For box.

   Your choices are:

   - On-screen Show—sets the width to 10 inches, the height to 7.5 inches, and the orientation to landscape (3:4 aspect ratio).

- Letter Paper (8.5 x 11 in)—sets the width to 10 inches, the height 7.5 inches, and the orientation to landscape so your slides fill the page. Select this size to print overhead transparencies (3:4 aspect ratio).

- A4 Paper (210 x 297 mm)—sets the width to 26 cm (10.83 inches) and the height to 18 cm (7.5 inches) if the orientation is landscape so that your slides fill A4 paper. (The aspect ratio is between that for on-screen and that for 35 mm.)

- 35mm Slides—sets the width to 11.25 inches and the height to 7.5 inches so that your content will fill the slide area in landscape orientation (2:3 aspect ratio).

- Custom—allows you to pick the dimensions you want by clicking the up or down arrow in the Width and Height boxes.

3. Under Orientation, use the Slides box to choose the orientation you want for your slides. In portrait orientation, the image is taller than it is wide; in landscape orientation, the image is wider than it is tall.

4. Under Orientation, use the Notes, Handouts, Outline box to choose the orientation you want for your notes, handouts, and outlines.

   You can choose to print notes, handouts, and outlines in a portrait orientation even if you've selected landscape orientation for your slides.

5. If you want to begin numbering your slides with a number other than 1, type that number in the Number Slides From box.

   Slide numbers appear on printed slides only when you insert them on a master by using the Page Number command on the Insert menu, the Page Number button, or by typing the symbol ##.

Printing the components of your presentation

The Print dialog box, accessible from the File menu, is where you specify what you want to print, the quantity, and any special print options.

▶ **To print slides, outlines, notes pages, and handouts**

1. From the File menu, choose Print.

   The Print dialog box appears.

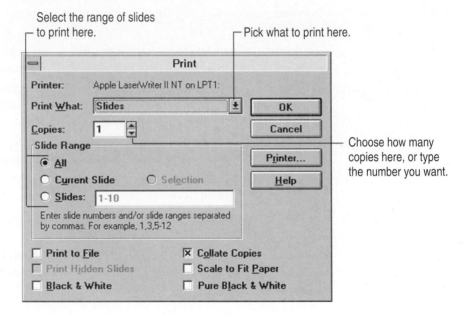

Select the range of slides to print here.

Pick what to print here.

Choose how many copies here, or type the number you want.

2. Select what you want to print in the Print What box.

   Your choices are:

   - Slides—prints your slides on paper or overhead transparencies, one image per page. (This option is available when there are no build slides.)

   - Slides (with builds)—prints each phase of a build slide as a separate page, starting with the title, then each major bullet item with its accompanying text. (This option is available only when the presentation includes build slides.)

   - Slides (without builds)—prints one page per build slide. (This option is available only when the presentation includes build slides.)

   - Notes Pages—prints the speaker's notes pages that correspond to the slide numbers you request.

   - Handouts (2 slides per page)—prints two slide images per page (use for the largest images and the greatest amount of detail).

- Handouts (3 slides per page)—prints three slide images per page (use when you want space for notes on one side of the page).

- Handouts (6 slides per page)—prints six slide images per page.

- Outline View—prints your outline according to how your outline appears on-screen in Outline view. An outline can be formatted or unformatted (plain text) and expanded or collapsed (titles only). Also, the type size depends on the view scale in which you are working.

3. In the Copies box, type the number of copies you want to print.

4. Select the range of slides or notes pages to be printed.

- All—prints all the slides in the presentation.

- Current Slide—prints the current slide or notes page.

- Slides—prints the range of slides or notes pages you specify. If you type only a beginning number, all slides or notes pages from that slide or notes page will be printed. If you want to print only one slide or notes page, type that slide's number in both boxes.

5. Choose any additional print options you want.

- Scale To Fit Paper—scales slides automatically to fit the paper loaded in your printer.

- Print Hidden Slides—prints all hidden slides. Otherwise, slides marked as hidden aren't printed.

- Pure Black & White—turns all color fills to white, all text and lines to black, adds outlines or borders to all filled objects, and renders pictures in grayscale. This option is useful when you want to print draft copies on a color printer or when you want to print very readable speaker's notes and handouts.

- Black & White—turns all fills to white (or black and white, if patterned). Unbordered objects that have no text appear with a thin black frame.

Additional options for Windows users:

- Print To File—"prints" the slides to a PostScript® file so they can be turned over to a service bureau to create 35mm slides or other materials.

  Print To File also allows you to print your presentation on another printer (the high-resolution one at work, for example) without having to install PowerPoint on it.

- Collate Copies—collates the pages when you print multiple copies of a presentation.

Additional options for Macintosh users:

- On the Print cascading menu, choose Black & White for quick black-and-white draft copies. Choose Color/Grayscale to print color on a color printer or grayscale images on a noncolor printer.

- In the Destination box, choose Printer to output to a printer. Choose PostScript File to "print" the slides to a PostScript file so they can be turned over to a service bureau to create 35mm slides or other materials.

6. Choose OK.

   Your selection prints.

Hints for printing

- Use the Print dialog box in conjunction with the Slide Setup dialog box. Paper size, print orientation, and slide numbering options are found in the Slide Setup dialog box; the number of copies is set in the Print dialog box.

- When you print 35mm slides as overhead transparencies, select the Scale To Fit Paper check box in the Print dialog box. PowerPoint scales your slides so they fit best on the transparencies.

- Your outline will always print to a width of 6.5 inches. The size of your text is determined by the current view size for Outline view. For example, in 50 percent view, 36-point text prints as 18-point.

- Each component has a master you can set up for printing. You can add footers, headers, notes, art, page numbers, and so on. For specifics, see "Working with the Slide Master" in Chapter 2, "Creating Presentations and Slides."

C H A P T E R   7

Using PowerPoint with Other Applications

There are several ways you can use PowerPoint with other applications, depending on what you want to do.

You can make use of the object linking and embedding (OLE) features in PowerPoint. If you *embed* an object—a chart from Microsoft Graph, for example—the object becomes a part of your PowerPoint presentation. You alone are the user of the data.

When you *link* an object—for example, a Microsoft Excel spreadsheet produced by the sales department—the object itself is stored in its source document, where it was created. Your PowerPoint presentation becomes one of several users of the data and can be automatically updated when others update the original spreadsheet. Your PowerPoint presentation stores only a representation of the original document.

The source worksheet

The worksheet is in a separate file linked to the PowerPoint presentation. Changes made to the worksheet file are reflected in the PowerPoint presentation when the link is updated.

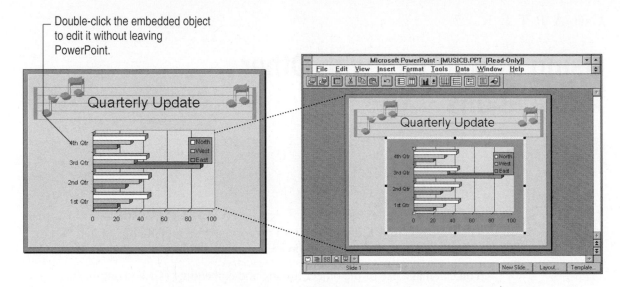

Double-click the embedded object to edit it without leaving PowerPoint.

The graph exists only as an object embedded in the PowerPoint presentation.

If you're a Macintosh user, you can also take advantage of the Publish and Subscribe commands to include data from other applications in your PowerPoint presentations. Generally, you *publish* an edition that's created in another application. Then, in PowerPoint, you *subscribe* to that edition.

That way, anytime you or another user of the data update the information in the original document, PowerPoint knows to update the edition that's in your presentation.

In This Chapter

Understanding Embedded and Linked Objects

Terms That Apply to Embedding and Linking

Embedded object An embedded object, such as a graph, a spreadsheet, or an organizational chart, is one that is created with another application but is stored in PowerPoint. Any updating you do to an embedded object is done manually while you are working in PowerPoint, provided you have the application that created it installed on your computer.

Linked object A linked object is also created in another application and maintains a connection to its source. Linked objects can be updated manually or automatically. If you choose to update automatically, then whenever the original object is changed, the linked object on the slide will also change. A linked object itself is stored in its source document, where it was created. Your PowerPoint presentation stores only a representation of the original document and information about its location.

Source document A source document is the file or document in which a linked object is created. A source document often resides on a network server, where many people can have access to it and can easily update its contents.

Container document The container document is the receiver of a linked object, which comes from the source document. A PowerPoint presentation that includes linked objects is a container document.

Object applications An object application is one in which you create an embedded object. It's the one to which you return to edit the embedded object.

In-place editing A feature of some object applications that allows direct editing of embedded objects on your PowerPoint slides, using the object application menus and toolbars.

Choosing Between Embedding and Linking

When choosing between embedding and linking, you need to consider how you're going to use the information in your presentation.

You would choose to embed an object when you're the *only* user of the information. An embedded object is one that is created by an application that can operate within other applications. Microsoft WordArt and Microsoft Graph can both operate within PowerPoint, for example. When you create a chart with Graph 5.0, you can update the chart while working in PowerPoint.

If you plan to show your presentation on other computers not on your network, you'll want to embed objects.

You'll want to create linked objects when the information or objects you're including in your presentation are likely to change and your presentation needs to have the latest version available. Or, if the information is being shared among documents or among users on a network, you'll want to link to the source.

Use these general guidelines to help decide between embedding and linking.

When you want to	Use this method	Comment
Include information that becomes part of your PowerPoint presentation, and that is always available even if the original source document is moved or erased.	Embed the objects from another application in the PowerPoint presentation.	To edit the object, the application that was used to create the object must be installed on the computer you're using.
Include a document that may not always be available, such as a document stored on a network server.	Embed the document from another application in the presentation.	
Include data maintained in a separate document. The PowerPoint presentation reflects any changes made to the document.	Create a link between the PowerPoint slide and the source document.	You store only the link, keeping the size of the presentation manageable. However, the link won't be available if you show the presentation on another computer unless you also transfer the source document.
Include a very large document, such as a video clip or sound clip.	Create a link between the PowerPoint slide and the source document.	You store only the link, keeping the size of the presentation manageable. However, the link won't be available if you show the presentation on another computer unless you also transfer the source document.

Working with Embedded Objects

An embedded object is one that is created by an object application and inserted into your presentation, using object linking and embedding. Once embedded, the information, which is now considered an *object*, becomes part of your PowerPoint presentation. Any updating you do to the embedded object is done while working in PowerPoint. Depending on what application created the object, when you double-click the object either a separate window opens in PowerPoint or some of the PowerPoint menus and toolbars are replaced by the ones in the object application.

You can embed an object you or someone else has already created—say a graph, special text effects created with WordArt, or a spreadsheet. Once you embed an object, you'll find it easy to go back and edit it.

You can recolor, resize, and crop embedded objects in PowerPoint. Special recoloring options are available for graphs and organizational charts, allowing PowerPoint to automatically recolor them to follow the color scheme or just the background and text colors. You can select either of these two options. Then when you change colors in PowerPoint, the embedded graph or chart is recolored accordingly.

You can add an embedded object to a PowerPoint presentation in a variety of ways. You can open an AutoLayout that includes an object placeholder; you can click a button on the Standard toolbar; or you use the Insert Object command on the Insert menu.

You can embed an object you or someone else has already created, as long as you have that object's application on your computer. You can also create a new object to embed in your presentation.

If you need help while working within the supplementary application, press the F1 key (Windows) or the HELP key (Macintosh) to open that application's Help system.

Here are some of the embedded objects you can add to your PowerPoint presentations:

- Text with special effects (created using Microsoft WordArt)
- Equations (from Microsoft Equation Editor)
- All types of charts (from Microsoft Graph)
- Organizational charts (from Microsoft Organization Chart)
- Tables (from Microsoft Word 6.0)
- Worksheets (from Microsoft Excel 5.0)

For more information about inserting embedded objects, see Chapter 5, "Adding Visuals to Slides."

How to Work with Embedded Objects

Embedding an existing object

You can choose to embed an object you or someone else has already created. By embedding it, you'll be able to edit the object later if you have the object's application on your computer.

There are three ways to embed an existing object in a PowerPoint presentation:

- You can open the object application and copy the object and then use the Paste Special command on the Edit menu to insert it into PowerPoint.

- You can save the object as a file in the object application and then use the Insert Object command to insert the file into PowerPoint.

- You can drag an embedded object from one PowerPoint presentation to another or from another application into PowerPoint if that application supports the drag-and-drop feature.

▶ **To embed an existing object**

1. Display the slide to which you want to add an embedded object.

2. From the Insert menu, choose Object.

   –or–

   Double-click an empty object placeholder on the current slide.

   The Insert Object dialog box appears.

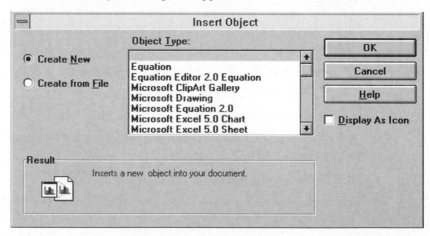

3. Select the Create From File option button.

   The Object Type box changes to the File box.

4. Type the name of the file you want to embed, and then choose OK.

    −or−

    Choose the Browse button, go to the file's directory and select it, and then choose OK.

5. Do one of the following:

    -   If the application offers in-place editing, click away from the object (Windows).

    -   If the object was created in another application with its own window, from the File menu, choose Exit And Return (Windows) or Quit And Update (Macintosh).

Creating an embedded object

When you create an embedded object, you open the object application within PowerPoint, make the object, and then embed it in your presentation.

When you're creating the object, you're working in the object application's work area. When you return to PowerPoint, only the object you created in the work area is transferred to PowerPoint.

▶ **To create an embedded object**

1. Display the slide to which you want to add an embedded object.

2. From the Insert menu, choose Object.

    −or−

    Double-click the object-specific placeholder.

    −or−

    Double-click an empty object-specific placeholder.

    The Insert Object dialog box appears.

3. Select the Create New option button.

4. In the Object Type box, select the application you want to use to create the object, and then choose OK.

    The object application, its work area, and its menus appear.

5. Use the tools and menu commands to create the object you want to embed.

6. When you finish working on the object, return to PowerPoint—and embed the object in your presentation—by doing one of the following:

    -   If the application temporarily replaces some of the PowerPoint menus and toolbars (called in-place editing), click anywhere in the PowerPoint window (Windows).

    -   If you created the object in another application that's in a separate window, choose Exit And Return (Windows) or Quit And Update (Macintosh).

Tip   You can also click the application buttons to create and embed objects in PowerPoint presentations. There are buttons for Microsoft Excel, Microsoft Organization Chart, Microsoft Graph, Microsoft Word, and others on the Standard toolbar. When you do this, you skip the Insert Object dialog box and go directly to the application.

Editing an embedded object

Most of the time, you only need to double-click an embedded object to open its creating application and to begin editing it. At other times you might find it necessary to use the commands on the Edit menu.

For some applications, part of the PowerPoint window is temporarily covered by the work area and menus of the object application (called in-place editing); for other applications, a separate window opens, containing the object in its original application.

Tip   You can see a shortcut menu of the commands you can use with an embedded object by clicking the right mouse button (Windows) or pressing COMMAND+click (Macintosh).

Some applications, such as Microsoft WordArt, open a separate window within the PowerPoint window. When you're finished editing, from the File menu, choose Exit And Return (Windows) or Quit And Update (Macintosh).

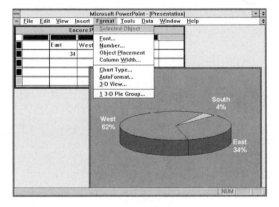

Other applications, such as Microsoft Graph, allow in-place editing. Their menus and toolbars replace the PowerPoint menus and toolbars. When you finish editing, click on the slide away from the object.

▶ **To edit an embedded object**

1. Double-click the embedded object.

   −or−

   Select the object and, from the Edit menu, choose [*Object*], and then choose Edit from the cascading menu.

   Sometimes you'll see both an Edit command and an Open command. Choose Open to edit the object in its own application window, or choose Edit to edit the object in the PowerPoint window.

2. Edit the object using its application's menus and tools.

3. When you're finished making your changes, return to PowerPoint by doing one of the following:

   ▪ If you're doing in-place editing in an application that temporarily replaces the PowerPoint menus and toolbars (Windows), click anywhere outside the embedded object to return to PowerPoint.

   ▪ If you're working in a separate application window, from the File menu, choose Exit And Return (Windows) or Quit And Update (Macintosh).

Converting an embedded object to a different format

You can convert an embedded object to a different file format by selecting another application to be the object's application. For example, if you want to edit a Lotus® 1-2-3® worksheet in your presentation but don't have Lotus 1-2-3 installed on your computer, you can specify another application to be the worksheet's source application.

▶ **To convert an embedded object to a different file format**

1. Select the object you want to convert.

2. From the Edit menu, choose the name of the object application.

   A cascading menu appears showing you the editing options available for the kind of object you are working on.

3.   From the cascading menu, choose Convert.

The Convert dialog box appears.

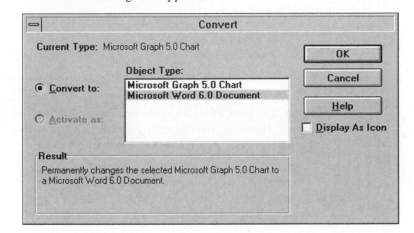

The available formats you can convert your file to are listed in the Object Type box.

4.   To *permanently* convert the selected embedded object to the format you select in the Object Type box, choose the Convert To option button.

−or−

To *temporarily* work with the embedded object using a different format, choose the Activate As option button, if it is available.

By choosing Activate As, you temporarily convert the embedded object you've selected, as well as all of the objects of the same kind within your presentation. When you finish editing and return to PowerPoint, the object or objects revert to their original file format.

5.   In the Object Type list, select the format to which you want to convert the object, and choose OK.

Converting an embedded object into a PowerPoint object

Many embedded objects—organizational charts, graphs, WordArt, and so on— can be converted into PowerPoint objects and can then be edited using PowerPoint tools. Converting an embedded object into a picture greatly reduces the amount of disk space used by the object. However, once you do this, you lose any link the object had with its original application. Converting an object is useful if you know you aren't going to continue updating the object.

▶   **To convert an embedded object into a PowerPoint object**

1.   Select the object you want to convert to a PowerPoint object.

2. From the Draw menu, choose Ungroup.

   PowerPoint will ask if you're sure you want to sever the object's link with its original application.

3. Choose OK.

   The object ungroups, and you can now work with its separate parts.

4. If you want to make the component parts whole again, from the Draw menu, choose Regroup.

   The object is grouped again, and you can move it, cut and paste it, or copy it as you want. However, the object is no longer linked with its original application, and you can't convert it back to an embedded object.

Tip You can also copy the object in its original application, and then switch to PowerPoint and paste it as a picture onto a slide by using the Paste Special command on the Edit menu. In the Paste Special dialog box, choose Picture.

Working with Linked Objects (Windows)

Let's say you're creating a presentation for the sales department. You'll be including sales data from various regions of the country, and you want to be able to use the latest figures available. The sales department stores its information on a Microsoft Excel worksheet. You can link a slide in your presentation to the sales department's worksheet and specify that the chart in your presentation be updated each time the sales department changes its figures. This way, you know that each time you show your presentation, you are including the latest available information.

When you link information in your PowerPoint presentation, you can choose automatic updating; each time you open the presentation, the information is automatically updated. Or you can decide to check the data first and then update with a keystroke.

You can convert the information into a PowerPoint object and edit it using the PowerPoint menus and toolbars. However, once you break the link, any updating you do to the original has no effect on the object in your presentation.

Note If you're a Microsoft Word user, you might be used to different terms. What Word and some other applications consider a "selection" is called an "object" in PowerPoint. Also, in Word you can convert an embedded object into a graphic. In PowerPoint, you can do likewise, but you convert the embedded object into a PowerPoint object.

You can bring lots of different kinds of visuals and information into your PowerPoint presentations as linked objects. The application in which you create the object just needs to support object linking and embedding. For instance, you can link to objects such as these:

- Movies (from Media Player for Windows or from QuickTime for Macintosh)
- Excel charts (from Microsoft Excel)
- PowerPoint objects and slides from other presentations (from PowerPoint for Windows)
- Organizational charts (from Microsoft Organization Chart)

How to Work with Linked Objects

Creating a link

There are two ways to create a link: by copying and pasting an object, or by using the Object command on the Insert menu. You can copy information in another application and then paste it into your PowerPoint slide using the Paste Special command on the Edit menu. Using the Object command, you can create a link to an object without leaving PowerPoint.

▶ **To create a link to an object**

1. Make sure you've saved the file in which the object was created before you set up the link to the object.

2. Open the object application, and select the information/object you want to link.

3. From the Edit menu, choose Copy.

4. Open the PowerPoint presentation in which you want to insert the object, and display the slide on which you want the object to appear.

5. From the Edit menu, choose Paste Special.

The Paste Special dialog box appears.

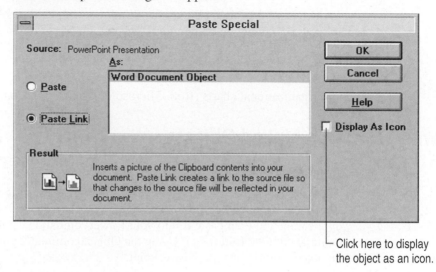

— Click here to display
the object as an icon.

If the object's format allows a link to be created, then the Paste Link option will be available.

6. Choose the Paste Link option button.

7. Select the format you want in the As box if you have a choice.

The object appears on the slide and the link is established to the source document so that the linked object will automatically be updated.

Tip You can save time when you open a PowerPoint presentation that includes many linked objects by choosing to update them manually rather than automatically. This is especially useful if the linked objects won't be changing much. If links are updated automatically, PowerPoint will update all the linked objects before allowing you to work on your presentation.

▶ **To create a link to another document without leaving PowerPoint**

1. From the Insert menu, choose Object.

The Insert Object dialog box appears.

2. Select Create From File.

3. In the File box, type or select the name of the file to which you want to link.

4. Select the Link check box, and then choose OK.

Changing the way a link works

The Links command on the Edit menu displays the Links dialog box. Here's where you change the properties of the link you have set up between the container and the object documents. In the Links dialog box, you can change the source of the link, you can break the link, or you can change the way the link is updated.

▶ **To change the way a link works**

1. From the Edit menu, choose Links.

    The Links dialog box appears.

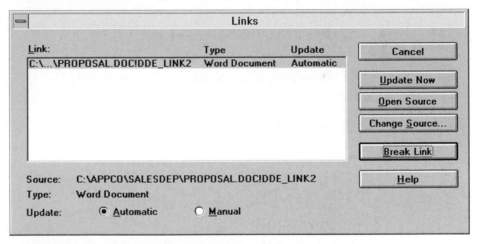

    Under Link is a list of the linked objects in your presentation.

2. Select the link whose properties you want to change.

3. Use the dialog box controls to change the link:

    - To update the linked object anytime you open the presentation, select the Automatic option button. (This is the default.)

    - To update manually by clicking Update Now, select the Manual option button or choose Update Links from the shortcut menu.

    - To update the linked object right now, whether it was created to link automatically or manually, choose the Update Now button.

- To cancel the link, so that changes in the original will no longer be reflected in the linked copy, choose the Break Link button.

  A picture of the linked object remains in your presentation.

- To change the link (for example, to reestablish a link after the original document has been moved), choose the Change Source button. A Directory dialog box opens in which you can enter the location of the document to be linked.

- To edit the linked object in the object's creating application, choose the Open Source button.

▶ **To update a link manually**

1. From the Edit menu, choose Links.

   The Links dialog box appears.

2. Under Link, select the link you want to update.

3. Choose the Update Now button.

Breaking a link

When you break a link, the linked object remains in your document as a picture, but it can no longer be updated. Once you break the link, you can't reconnect it. To reestablish a link, you must delete the unlinked object from your slide and create a new link.

▶ **To break a link**

1. From the Edit menu, choose Links.

   The Links dialog box appears.

2. Under Link, select the link or links you want to cancel.

3. Choose the Break Link button, and then answer Yes when a message box appears and asks whether you want to cancel the link.

Editing linked information

You need to edit linked information in its object application, which you can open while working in PowerPoint.

▶ **To edit linked information**

1. Double-click the object you want to edit.

   –or–

   Select it, and, from the Edit menu, choose [*Object*] (name of the linked object's application), and then, from the cascading menu, choose Edit.

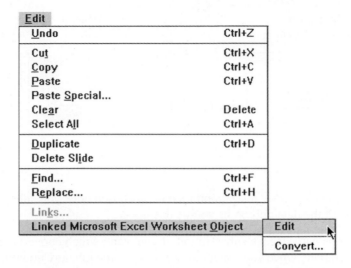

When you want to edit a Microsoft Excel worksheet, choose Microsoft Excel Worksheet Object from the Edit menu, and then choose Edit from the cascading menu.

The source document opens.

2. In the source document, make the changes you want.

3. When you're finished, from the File menu, choose Exit.

Publishing and Subscribing (Macintosh)

The Publish and Subscribe To commands on the Macintosh let you create an object in one application, then import it into your PowerPoint presentation.

When you create a publisher, you're saving a section of a document as an edition that you (or others) can use in other documents, such as your PowerPoint presentation. You can both publish and subscribe to individual PowerPoint slides. You can also subscribe to editions created in applications other than PowerPoint. The most significant feature of a subscriber is that it retains an active connection with its publisher through the edition; when changes are made to the publisher, the edition is updated and the changes are made to the subscriber.

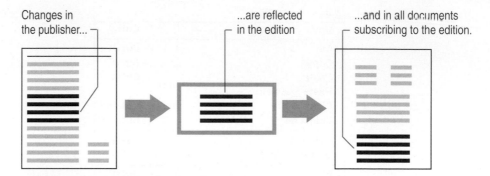

You can move, resize, and recolor an edition once you subscribe to it, but you can edit the data only in its source document.

You can cancel a subscription, if you want, which converts the object to a graphic. Once you cancel a subscription, though, any updating you do to the publisher will not affect the object in your presentation.

You can publish a PowerPoint slide and subscribe to it in another document—a Microsoft Word file, for instance—or in another PowerPoint presentation. When publishing PowerPoint slides, remember that you must publish the *entire* slide, not just part of it.

Terms That Apply to Publishing and Subscribing

Publisher   The publisher is the source document that creates an object you place in a PowerPoint presentation. Whenever a publisher is changed, the object in your presentation will be updated.

Edition   The edition is the object that is created in the source document, or the publisher. It's the edition that you put on your PowerPoint slide. The edition is linked to the source document, so that whenever the original is changed, the changes are reflected in the presentation.

Subscriber   The subscriber is the document that receives an edition from the publisher. PowerPoint can be a subscriber to an edition.

How to Work with Publishers and Subscribers

Creating a publisher and an edition

You use the Create Publisher command to publish slides from your PowerPoint presentation. You can edit a publisher the same way you edit other parts of a document.

▶ **To publish a slide and create an edition**

1. Open the presentation that contains the slide you want to publish.

   Make sure you save the presentation containing the slide you want to publish or the edition won't be connected.

2. In Slide Sorter view, select the slide you want in the edition.

   You must select the entire slide. You can't publish individual objects within a slide.

3. From the Edit menu, choose Create Publisher.

   The Create Publisher dialog box appears.

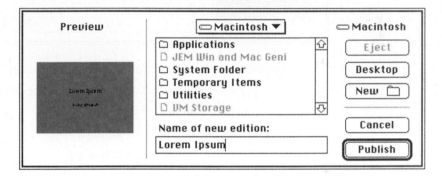

The Preview box shows the beginning of the publisher.

4. Type a name for the edition in the Name Of New Edition box.

5. Choose the Publish button.

   The edition material you selected is published and saved in the edition you named.

Subscribing to an edition

When you subscribe to an edition, you insert a copy of the edition into your PowerPoint presentation. Once you have inserted an edition into the subscriber, updates received by the edition are automatically sent to the subscriber. As long as the edition remains available to PowerPoint, the connection is maintained between the edition and the subscriber, even if you change the name of either the edition or the subscriber.

▶ **To subscribe to a slide**

1. Create an edition of the slide to which you want to subscribe.

2. Open the PowerPoint presentation in which you want to insert a published slide.

3. In Slide or Notes view, display the slide on which you want to insert a published edition.

4. From the Edit menu, choose Subscribe To.

The Subscribe To dialog box appears.

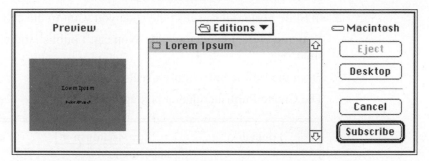

5. Select the edition you want to insert in your presentation.

You'll see a preview of the selected edition in the Preview box.

6. Choose the Subscribe button.

The edition you selected appears on the slide.

You can move or resize the object if you want.

Updating an edition

Once you've created a publisher and an edition, you can specify how frequently you want to update the edition with changes you make to the publisher. Unless you specify otherwise, PowerPoint updates the edition as soon as you save changes to the publisher.

▶ **To control how an edition is updated**

1. Select the publisher for which you want to change the update frequency.

2. From the Edit menu, choose Publisher Options.

The Publisher Options dialog box appears.

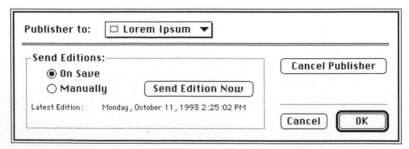

3. Under Send Editions, choose one of the following.

To update the edition	Do this
Whenever you save the publisher	Select the On Save option button.
Only when you choose the Send Edition Now button	Select the Manually option button.
Whenever you make changes to the publisher	Select the On Save option button, and then select the Send Edition When Edited check box.

4. Choose the OK button.

▶ **To send an edition manually**

1. Select the publisher you want to update.

2. From the Edit menu, choose Publisher Options.

3. Choose the Send Edition Now button.

4. Choose the OK button.

Canceling a Publisher

If you decide you no longer need to update the edition in your presentation, you can cancel the publisher. The contents of the edition remain in your presentation. Meanwhile, other users can still subscribe to the edition. Because you'll no longer need the edition, you can delete it in the Finder, just as you would delete any other file.

▶ **To cancel a publisher**

1. Open the document that contains the publisher you want to cancel, and then position the insertion point in the publisher.

2. From the Edit menu, choose Publisher Options.

   The Publisher Options dialog box appears.

3. Choose the Cancel Publisher button.

   PowerPoint asks you to confirm that you want to cancel the publisher.

Updating a subscriber

Once you've subscribed to an edition, you can specify how frequently you want to receive updates. Unless you choose another option, PowerPoint assumes you want the subscriber automatically updated as soon as a new edition is available.

▶ **To control how a subscriber is updated**

1. Select the subscriber.

2. From the Edit menu, choose Subscriber Options.

3. Under Get Editions, do one of the following.

To update the subscriber	Choose
Whenever a change is made in the edition	The Automatically button
Only when you specify	The Manually button

Note Changing the update frequency of the subscriber affects only how often the subscriber receives updates from the edition, not how frequently the publisher sends updates to the edition.

▶ **To update a subscriber manually**

1. Select the subscriber you want to update.

2. From the Edit menu, choose Subscriber Options.

3. Choose the Get Edition Now button.

Editing a publisher

If you need to change the contents or formatting of a subscriber, it's best to make the changes in the publisher itself. This way, the changes will be reflected in the subscriber.

▶ **To edit a publisher**

1. Select the publisher you want to edit.

2. From the Edit menu, choose Subscriber Options.

3. Choose the Open Publisher button.

   PowerPoint opens the publisher you want to edit.

4. Make the changes to the publisher.

5. When you're finished editing, save and close the publisher document. Each subscriber reflects the changes you've made, depending on the update options for the publisher and subscriber.

Editing an edition

You may find you don't have access to the publisher when you want to make changes—the publisher may be a read-only document. If this is the case, you can make changes to the edition, which will then be reflected in your presentation.

▶ **To access the edition for editing**

1. Double-click the object in your presentation.

   –or–

2. Select the object, and then, from the Edit menu, choose Edit Subscriber.

   The edition file opens in the application in which it was created.

3. Make any changes you want, and then, from the file menu, choose Quit.

4. The subscriber is updated when you return to PowerPoint.

Canceling a subscriber

You might find you no longer have access to a publisher, or that you don't need to receive updated information from an edition. You can cancel the subscriber, and then you are free to edit the information in PowerPoint.

▶ **To cancel a subscriber**

1. Select the subscriber you want to cancel.

2. From the Edit menu, choose Subscriber Options.

   The Subscriber Options dialog box appears.

3. Choose Cancel Subscriber.

4. PowerPoint asks you to confirm that you want to cancel the subscriber. Choose OK.

Sending Mail

If you see the Send command (Windows) or the Mail command (Macintosh) on the File menu, Microsoft Mail is installed. That means you can send your presentations to someone using electronic mail. You can either send a presentation to one person or you can route a presentation to more than one person, using the Add Routing Slip command (Windows) or the Add Slip on the Mail cascading menu (Macintosh).

To send and route presentations, the sender and the receiver(s) must have PowerPoint and Microsoft Mail or another compatible mail package installed.

How to Send and Route Mail

Sending a presentation

You can send mail without using a routing slip when you're just sending a presentation directly to another person. The presentation is saved as an attachment to a note.

▶ **To send a presentation to another PowerPoint user**

1. From the File menu, choose Send (Windows) or Mail and then Send from the Mail cascading menu (Macintosh).

   A dialog box appears so you can identify the person who is to receive your presentation.

   For detailed instructions, see the online Help system in Microsoft Mail.

2. When you've completed the address information, choose Send.

Routing a presentation

You can send one or more copies of the same presentation to others for their review. For example, you might want a small group to review an important presentation before you give it.

▶ **To route a presentation to other PowerPoint users**

1. Open the presentation you want to route.

2. From the File menu, choose Add Routing Slip.

   If you are editing an existing slip, the command changes to Edit Routing Slip.

3. Choose the Address button.

4. Select the names of those to whom you want to route the presentation, choose Add, and then choose OK.

   If you want to route the presentation to one recipient after another, use the Move Up and Move Down arrows to put the names in the correct routing order.

5. In the Subject and Message Text boxes, type the subject and any message you want to send with the presentation.

   The same message goes to all recipients.

   PowerPoint automatically adds instructions telling recipients to choose the Send command when they are finished.

6. Under Route To Recipients, do one of the following:

   ▪ To route one copy of a presentation to one recipient after another, select the One After Another option button.

   ▪ To route multiple copies of a presentation to all recipients at the same time, select the All At Once option button.

7. Choose any other options you want, and then choose the Route button.

   For more information on other options, see the online Help system in Microsoft Mail.

8. When you are ready to send the presentation, choose Route.

   PowerPoint displays a message asking you to confirm that you want to route the presentation.

Recipients can change the presentation and route it to the next recipient or return the copy to you by choosing Send from the File menu.

Inserting a Movie

You can use Media Player (Windows) or QuickTime (Macintosh) to play movies in your PowerPoint presentation. The Media Player comes with the Windows version of PowerPoint. Macintosh PowerPoint users will get QuickTime as part of the Macintosh system.

A movie appears on a slide as a poster frame—usually a picture of the first frame of the movie. You start your movie manually by double-clicking the icon or set it to run automatically as you give a slide show on your computer. You can choose to run the movie once or have it run in a continuous loop during a show.

Refer to the Help system for the Microsoft Media Player (Windows) to find out about the features and functions available to you as you work with movies.

How to Work with Movies

Inserting a movie

▶ **To insert a movie (Windows)**

1. From the Insert menu, choose Object, and then select Media Clip in the Object Type box.

   −or−

   Double-click an object placeholder on an AutoLayout, and then choose Media Clip in the Object type box.

   The Media Player opens.

2. From the File menu, choose Open.

3. Select the movie file you want to insert.

4. From the File menu, choose Exit And Return.

   You return to your PowerPoint presentation.

▶ **To insert a movie (Macintosh)**

1. From the Insert menu, choose Movie.

   A dialog box appears in which you can select the movie you want to insert on the slide.

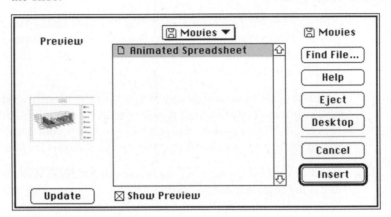

2. Select the movie, and then choose the Insert button.

Running a movie

You can preset a movie to run during your presentation. You can choose either an automatic start or a manual start. The default setting for movies is to play on a mouse click and automatically after the slide transition. Movies are set to stop on a mouse click, when the movie is over, or when you go to the next slide, whichever comes first.

▶ **To change play settings for a movie (Windows and Macintosh)**

1. Select the movie for which you want to change the play settings.

2. From the Tools menu, choose Play Settings.

The Play Settings dialog box appears.

This is the Play Settings dialog box (Windows).

3. In the Start Play box, choose one of the following:

- **When Click On Object**—This choice allows you to begin the movie manually by clicking the object's icon. (This is the default.)

- **When Transition Starts**—This means that the movie will begin as the transition to the slide begins.

- **When Transition Ends Plus [*blank*] Seconds**—This choice allows you to set a number of seconds after the transition to the slide ends. To activate this option, type in the number of seconds you want to wait until the movie begins.

Editing a movie

Sometimes you'll want to edit a movie—cut some frames, for instance, or adjust the volume. You do this working in Slide view and using the movie controller.

Tip   You can use the special option for scaling movies in the Scale dialog box to resize movies proportionally in PowerPoint.

▶ **To edit a movie (Windows)**

1. In Slide view, go to the slide that contains the movie icon, and then select it.

2. From the Edit menu, choose Edit Media Clip Object, and then choose Edit from the cascading menu.

The Media Player opens.

3. Edit the movie as needed.

4. When you're finished making changes, from the File menu, choose Update.

5. From the File menu in Media Player, choose Exit.

   The Media Player closes, and you return to PowerPoint.

▶ **To edit a QuickTime movie (Macintosh)**

1. In Slide view, go to the slide that contains the movie icon.

2. From the Edit menu, choose Edit Movie, and then choose Show Controller.

   Or click the movie icon (also called the movie badge) to show the controller.

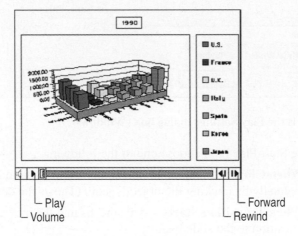

⌐ Play
⌐ Volume

⌐ Forward
⌐ Rewind

3. Edit the movie.

Here are the basic ways you can control a movie.

Controlling a QuickTime Movie

To do this	Do this
Stop a movie and return to the presentation	Click outside the movie.
Pause the current frame	Click in the movie.
	–or–
	Click the Play/Pause button.
Restart from the current frame	Double-click in the movie.
Advance one frame	Click the Forward button.
Go back one frame	Click the Rewind button.
Advance/rewind several frames	Drag the Slider forward/backward.
Loop the movie when played	Choose Movie from the Edit menu; choose Loop from the cascading menu.
Change the movie poster	With the frame you want displayed, choose Movie from the Edit menu; choose Set As Poster Frame.
Adjust the volume	Click the Volume button, and then drag the volume control up or down.
Cut or copy a single frame	With the frame displayed, choose Cut or Copy from the Edit menu.
Cut or copy a sequence of frames	With the first frame displayed, hold down the SHIFT key and drag until all frames you want are selected. Choose Cut or Copy from the Edit menu.

A P P E N D I X   A

Installing and Using PowerPoint on a Network

This appendix discusses how to install and use PowerPoint for Windows on a network.

The first section, "Setting up PowerPoint on a Network File Server," is for network administrators who install PowerPoint on the network. Before installing PowerPoint on any network workstations, the network administrator must install PowerPoint on a network file server or a shared directory.

The second section, "Creating Custom Installations for Workstation Users," is for network administrators who want to create custom installation scripts that workstation users can run to install or upgrade PowerPoint.

The final section, "Network Considerations for Workstation Users," is for PowerPoint users who run PowerPoint from a network file server. It also includes information for users in workgroups.

Designating Network Connections

In this appendix network connections are specified with a logical drive letter, such as N. If your network supports the use of universal naming convention (UNC) paths of the form \\server\share, you can use a path instead of a logical drive letter. Setup remembers the paths to the components you install, so if you use logical drive letters to specify network file servers during installation, you have to make those network connections manually and use the same drive letters before you run Setup again. If you use UNC paths, Setup will make the correct connections automatically.

> **Note** Every PowerPoint user must have a Microsoft PowerPoint license. A license is obtained by buying a retail package or a Microsoft License Pak. For more information about network use restrictions, see your Microsoft PowerPoint license agreement.

Setting Up PowerPoint on a Network File Server

This section is for network administrators who perform an administrator's installation on a network file server or a shared directory.

Users on networks can share the PowerPoint program and documents created in PowerPoint. Once you've installed PowerPoint on the network, a workstation user can either install the program and its components on the workstation's hard disk or run PowerPoint from the network file server.

This appendix assumes that you know how to use network software to connect to network drives and how to find files stored on network file servers.

Before you set up PowerPoint on a network file server, check the following:

- The network must be operational, and you must have read, write, and delete/erase privileges for the network directories in which you want to install PowerPoint. For more information, see your network software documentation.

- You must install the Windows operating system, version 3.1 or later, on the workstation you use to install PowerPoint on the network file server, and on any workstations that will run PowerPoint. For information about installing Windows, see your Windows documentation.

- If any network users share the Windows operating system or other applications, they must be logged off from the network. The directories that contain shared components on the file server or shared volume must be locked from user access—for example, W:\WINDOWS and W:\MSAPPS. You must have create, write, and delete privileges in these directories.

- You should determine in which network file server directories the components of PowerPoint should be installed. Setup suggests installing POWERPNT.EXE in the POWERPNT directory and installing shared components in the MSAPPS directory of the network file server or the shared volume. You can specify other paths if you want to.

Setting up PowerPoint on network workstations is a two-step process. First install PowerPoint on the network file server. Then set up the workstations, either by installing PowerPoint on each workstation's hard disk or by setting up the workstations to run PowerPoint from the file server.

Installation Requirements

If the file server or shared workstation can run Windows version 3.1, it can run PowerPoint, provided that it has sufficient RAM and disk space. Each workstation should have at least 4 MB of RAM and sufficient disk space for the PowerPoint program and the options you want to install.

▶ **To install PowerPoint for Windows on a network file server or a shared directory**

1. Ask all users who are sharing Windows or Microsoft applications such as PowerPoint and Microsoft Excel (which share components) to disconnect from the network file server or the shared directory.

2. Start Microsoft Windows, and quit any other applications.

3. Insert the disk labeled "Disk 1" in drive A or drive B.

4. From the File menu in either Program Manager or File Manager, choose Run.

5. Type *drive letter*:**setup** /**a** and then press ENTER. (The /a switch indicates an administrator's installation.)

6. Follow the instructions on the screens that Setup displays. You need to supply your company name, which will be included with workstation installations made from the file server. You will have one opportunity to confirm the company name. Make sure that the name is correct before you proceed; once you've confirmed it, you cannot change it.

   You also need to supply the network directory in which you want to install the main PowerPoint Program (for example, N:\POWERPNT), and the directory for storing shared components, such as Microsoft Graph and Microsoft WordArt. Shared components are usually stored in the MSAPPS directory at the same directory level as the directory that contains POWERPNT.EXE—for example, N:\MSAPPS.

   If you are running the Windows operating system from a shared installation, the proposed location for the shared components is at the same directory level as the shared Windows directory—for example, W:\MSAPPS.

   When users install PowerPoint on their workstations using this administrator's installation, the shared components can be installed locally or run from the network. Before you complete the administrator's installation, decide if the shared components will be automatically installed on individual workstations, automatically shared from the network, or if the choice will be left to the workstation user.

7. Set the access privileges to read-only for the server directories in which you installed PowerPoint components, and ensure that all users who may need to install PowerPoint on their workstations from the network have read privileges for those directories.

Creating Custom Installations for Workstation Users

You can create scripts to run Setup "silently" and control how Setup installs PowerPoint. With a script, you can do the following:

- Perform a complete installation automatically, without input from the user.
- Control which type of installation—Typical, Complete/Custom, or Laptop (Minimum)—you want Setup to perform.
- Specify the directory in which to install PowerPoint.
- Ensure that all installations in a workgroup are the same.

Setup uses information in the file SETUP.STF to determine which files to install and where they should be copied.

To perform a complete installation automatically, just add the /q switch when you run Setup. For example, switch to the server or directory where Setup is installed, and then type **setup /q** to start an automatic installation. When you use this switch, Setup reads information from SETUP.STF and installs PowerPoint in the program directory for the previous version of PowerPoint or in the default PowerPoint program directory, C:\POWERPNT, without prompting the user for information.

To control which type of installation Setup performs and specify the directory where PowerPoint is installed, edit SETUP.STF to create a custom script that workstation users can run to install PowerPoint.

Editing SETUP.STF to Create a Script

This section describes how to create a script that automatically performs a Typical, Complete/Custom, Laptop (Minimum), or Workstation installation and how to specify a directory where Setup will install PowerPoint.

You can also add information to SETUP.STF to install custom templates and other files that you want to be part of the standard installation for workstation users.

▶ **To edit the information in SETUP.STF**

1. Copy the file SETUP.STF from the directory in which you installed the main PowerPoint program. Open the copy of SETUP.STF (not the original) with any spreadsheet application, word processor, or text editor. It is easiest to work with the table in a spreadsheet application such as Microsoft Excel.

2. To specify the type of installation you want the script to perform, scroll through the table until you see the following list of installation options in the third column:
   - Typical
   - Complete/Custom

- Laptop (Minimum)
- Workstation

Type **yes** in the column labeled "Install During Batch Mode" to the left of the type of installation you want the script to perform. Type **no** next to the other options.

3. If you want the script to perform a Compete/Custom installation, scroll down until you see the following list of components in the third column:

- Microsoft PowerPoint Program Files
- Shared Applications
- Converters, Filters, and Translators
- Help, Quick Preview, and Cue Cards
- Templates
- Tools
- Clip Art Files
- PowerPoint Viewer

Type **yes** in the column to the left of each component you want the script to install. Type **no** next to the other options.

4. To specify a directory where Setup will install PowerPoint, scroll through the table until you see "Network Installation" in the third column. Replace the "%1" in the DestDir column of this row with the name of the directory where you want Setup to install PowerPoint.

5. Save the edited table in text-only format with the new name you assigned in Step 1.

Important To ensure that Setup works properly, do not edit any other part of the table file. If the initial value in a cell is empty, do not edit the cell. If you are using a text editor, do not delete tab characters that separate table columns.

Distributing and Using a Script

After you create a script, you can copy it to the file server or shared volume from which you want users to install PowerPoint, or you can distribute it with Microsoft Mail or another application that can send items across a network.

Use one of the following methods to distribute a script:

- Copy SETUP.EXE and give the copy the same filename you gave the script but use the .EXE filename extension. For example, if you named the script NEWSETUP.STF, name the copy of the Setup executable file NEWSETUP.EXE. Put the renamed setup file and the script on the file server or the shared volume. Direct your users to run the copy of the Setup executable file (for example, NEWSETUP.EXE, not SETUP.EXE).

- To create one script for all users, rename the SETUP.STF file that comes with PowerPoint to something else, such as SETUP.OLD. Name the script SETUP.STF, and save it in the same network directory as SETUP.EXE. Direct your users to run SETUP.EXE from the file server or the shared volume.

- To create different installation scripts for different groups of users, distribute the script with Microsoft Mail or another application as a Program Manager icon. The command line specifies the script and switches, as shown in the following table.

Switch	Instructions
/t tablename	Substitute the name of the new script for tablename.
/n username	(Optional) Substitute a value for username to prevent Setup from prompting the user for a name. The name must be enclosed in quotation marks as shown in the example that follows. To automatically register the workstation copy of PowerPoint with the workstation's existing user name, type the quotation marks with no name (""). Setup uses the name specified in the WIN.INI file on the workstation in the DefName line of the [MS User Info] section.
/q	Causes Setup to run without any user interaction.

For example, suppose you installed PowerPoint in the POWERPNT directory of a file server—where X designates the file server—and you want to distribute a silent script that uses the MYSCRIPT.STF table file to a user named Paul Tanner. The command line would be

```
x:\powerpnt\setup.exe /t myscript.stf /n "Paul Tanner" /q
```

Distributing a Script with Microsoft Mail

If you use Microsoft Mail to distribute a script, create a new message and then choose Insert Object from the Edit menu. In the Object Type box, select Package, and then choose the OK button. From the Edit menu in Object Packager, choose Command Line. Type the full path to SETUP.EXE in the POWERPNT directory of the file server or the shared directory. (If your network supports UNC pathnames, use that syntax. If not, users will need to make the network connection themselves by using the same drive letter you specified before running Setup.) Type **setup** and the following switches and arguments as needed, and then choose the OK button.

To attach the PowerPoint Setup icon to the command line, choose the Insert Icon button in Object Packager. Choose the Browse button to locate SETUP.EXE in the POWERPNT directory of the network file server, and then choose the OK button. Choose Update from the File menu to add the icon to the Mail message, and then choose Exit from the File menu to close Object Packager. The icon is now ready to distribute. Anyone who receives the message can double-click the icon to run Setup from the network and use the script you specified with the /t switch.

Network Considerations for Workstation Users

There are two ways to run PowerPoint in a network environment:

- You can run PowerPoint entirely off the network, without installing it on your own computer.

- You can install PowerPoint—in its entirety—on your own computer.

Installing PowerPoint on a Workstation

If your computer is connected to a network file server or a shared directory, your network administrator may have installed a copy of PowerPoint on the network that you can then install on your workstation. The administrator may also have created a process you can use to install PowerPoint automatically. Check with your administrator to determine the best way for you to install PowerPoint.

Once you have installed PowerPoint, read the following This section for important information about using PowerPoint in a network environment. You may also need special network software to manage and synchronize shared files on the file server. For more information, check with your network administrator.

Sharing and Protecting Documents on Networks

Using PowerPoint on a network is essentially the same as using PowerPoint on a stand-alone computer. On a network, however, you can use the network file server to store documents and exchange them with other users, so you may want to protect some documents from unauthorized access.

Things to Remember About Shared Documents

If your workgroup uses a standard set of templates to ensure consistency, do not use other templates when you're working on a shared document.

In order for everyone who works on a shared presentation to display and print it the same way, the fonts used in the presentation must be available on the other computers and printers in your workgroup.

If you use TrueType fonts in shared documents, however, the fonts can be embedded in documents so that others who do not have those fonts installed can still see and print them.

APPENDIX B

Detailed Information About Installing PowerPoint 4.0

PowerPoint Installation Options

You can choose several levels of installation, depending on how much hard disk space you have available in your computer. In the PowerPoint 4.0 Setup dialog box, you can choose Typical, Custom/Complete, or Laptop installation.

Typical Installation

If you choose Typical installation, the most commonly used PowerPoint components are installed, including the templates, typical clip art, and some basic TrueType fonts. The typical installation also includes supplementary applications such as the spelling checker, WordArt, and Graph.

Custom/Complete Installation

When you choose Custom/Complete, the Custom/Complete dialog box appears. You can choose just those options you want to install (Custom) or you can simply click Continue to install PowerPoint and all of its components (Complete).

Custom installation If you choose Custom installation, PowerPoint asks you which parts of the complete package you want to include and which you don't want installed. You'll know you have additional choices if the More Options button is available when you select an option in the Options box. For example, if you select Applets and then click the More Options button, you'll see that you can install Equation Editor, WordArt, Organization Chart, and ClipArt Gallery if you want. You can choose to include any or all of these applications. If you know you're not likely to use an application such as Equation Editor (to create scientific notation), just deselect it, and the application won't be installed.

By not installing certain components, you'll also save disk space. At the bottom of the Custom/Complete dialog box, PowerPoint keeps track of the space it needs for installation, as well as the space that's available on your hard disk.

Complete installation If you choose Complete installation, the entire PowerPoint program and all components are installed.

Laptop (Minimum) Installation

If you choose the Laptop (Minimum) installation option, you get the minimum set of PowerPoint installation options, which requires the least hard drive storage space.

Replacing a Previous Version of PowerPoint

If there is a previous version of PowerPoint on your system when you run the installation program, you can replace it or install PowerPoint version 4.0 in a different directory or folder.

If you choose to replace the earlier version of PowerPoint, the installation program handles "housekeeping" tasks. If you're a Windows user, the installation program takes care of removing obsolete sections of the WIN.INI file, updating changed components, and so on. All of your existing files, including custom dictionaries and glossaries, can be opened normally in your new version of PowerPoint.

If you choose to install PowerPoint version 4.0 in a different place and keep the previous version of PowerPoint as well, the installation program doesn't change the existing templates, PowerPoint files, and so on.

Adding and Removing Components

Once you've installed PowerPoint, you can run Setup again at any time to add or remove any PowerPoint component. If you have already installed a component but PowerPoint can't find or use it properly, you can run Setup to remove it and then run Setup again to reinstall it in the appropriate place.

You can also run Setup to remove PowerPoint. Most of the PowerPoint files and entries added to WIN.INI and REG.DAT (Windows) or the System Folder (Macintosh) are removed. (Setup cannot remove all of the files it installed, because some of them may be required by other applications.)

Note If you uninstall PowerPoint components, you may have empty directories that you'll need to delete manually.

▶ **To add or remove individual components of PowerPoint**

1. Do one of the following:
   - On a stand-alone computer, double-click the PowerPoint Setup icon in the Program Manager (Windows) or Desktop (Macintosh). You'll find it in the same group in which you placed the PowerPoint icon.

- In the File Manager, double-click SETUP.EXE in the SETUP subdirectory of the PowerPoint program directory (Windows) or folder (Macintosh). If you originally set up PowerPoint from a network file server or a shared directory, run that copy of Setup. (If you're not running Setup from a network file server or a shared directory or folder, and you can't find Setup in the PowerPoint Program directory or folder on your computer, use the Setup disk that came with PowerPoint.)

The PowerPoint Installation Maintenance program dialog box appears.

2. You can choose the Add/Remove button, the Reinstall button, or the Remove All button.

   - If you choose the Add/Remove button, the Maintenance Installation dialog box appears and displays all of the available PowerPoint options. The selected options are the ones that are installed on your computer. Select items to add, or cancel items by removing the check.

   - If you choose the Reinstall button, Setup will reinstall PowerPoint as it was installed the last time you installed or reinstalled it. This option is useful if, for example, your WIN.INI entries have become corrupted or you have accidentally deleted a file.

   - If you choose the Remove All button, Setup will remove all PowerPoint components. Some components are shared by applications, and you may not want to remove these. Setup will ask if shared components should be removed.

3. Select the additional options you want to install or cancel the options you want to remove.

4. If the Change Option button is available, you can choose to add or remove a part of an option.

   For instance, if you choose Change Option after you've selected TrueType Fonts, you'll see which of the seven available font families are installed on your computer. You can add or remove any of the font families, if you want.

5. When you're finished, choose the Continue button.

Manually Decompressing a File (Windows)

The files on the PowerPoint disks are compressed to save space and must be decompressed before you use them. You should use the Setup program to decompress and install files automatically. However, if you want to decompress a single file without running Setup, you can decompress and copy the file yourself. Note that some large files on the program disks are actually portions of much larger files that Setup combines during the installation process, so you cannot manually decompress every file on the program disks.

The filename extension of a compressed file usually ends with an underscore (_). When you decompress a file, you will need to provide a new filename.

To manually decompress a file, copy the DECOMP.EXE decompression utility on Disk 1 to your hard drive.

To decompress and copy the file	At the DOS prompt, type
To the same directory	**decomp** *filename*
To a different directory	**decomp** *filename path*

Filename is the name, including the path, of the compressed file. *Path* is the destination path for the file.

Changes Setup Makes to Your System (Windows)

When Setup installs PowerPoint on your system, it may need to change your WIN.INI, REG.DAT, and SYSTEM.INI files. The following changes are new to this version of PowerPoint:

- Setup adds or updates a line in the SYSTEM.INI file that loads the VSHARE.386 driver, which is required to run PowerPoint. VSHARE.386 lets you run more than one session of PowerPoint at a time and protects you from file management errors. This driver will work properly even if the SHARE.EXE program is run from AUTOEXEC.BAT or CONFIG.SYS.

- Setup does not add the PowerPoint program directory to the PATH statement in the AUTOEXEC.BAT file. However, you can update the path to include the directory where the main PowerPoint program file, POWERPNT.EXE, is stored. For more information on how to edit the AUTOEXEC.BAT file, see your MS-DOS documentation.

A P P E N D I X   C

PowerPoint Keyboard Shortcuts

Text Formatting

To do this	Windows shortcut	Macintosh shortcut
Change font	CTRL+SHIFT+F	COMMAND+SHIFT+F
Change point size	CTRL+SHIFT+P	COMMAND+SHIFT+P
Increase font size	CTRL+SHIFT+>	COMMAND+SHIFT+>
Decrease font size	CTRL+SHIFT+<	COMMAND+SHIFT+<
Bold	CTRL+B	COMMAND+B
Underline	CTRL+U	COMMAND+U
Italic	CTRL+I	COMMAND+I
Raise baseline	ALT+CTRL+SHIFT+>	COMMAND+OPTION+SHIFT+>
Lower baseline	ALT+CTRL+SHIFT+<	COMMAND+OPTION+SHIFT+<
Plain text	CTRL+SHIFT+Z	COMMAND+SHIFT+Z
Center paragraph	CTRL+E	COMMAND+E
Justified paragraph	CTRL+J	COMMAND+J
Left-aligned paragraph	CTRL+L	COMMAND+L
Right-aligned paragraph	CTRL+R	COMMAND+R

Deleting and Copying

To do this	Windows shortcut	Macintosh shortcut
Delete character left	BACKSPACE	DEL
Delete word left	CTRL+BACKSPACE	COMMAND+BACKSPACE
Delete character right	DELETE	DEL
Delete word right	CTRL+DELETE	COMMAND+DEL
Cut	CTRL+X	COMMAND+X
Copy	CTRL+C	COMMAND+C
Paste	CTRL+V	COMMAND+V
Undo	CTRL+Z	COMMAND+Z

Navigating

To do this	Windows shortcut	Macintosh shortcut
Character left	LEFT ARROW	LEFT ARROW
Character right	RIGHT ARROW	RIGHT ARROW
Line up	UP ARROW	UP ARROW
Line down	DOWN ARROW	DOWN ARROW
Word left	CTRL+LEFT ARROW	OPTION+LEFT ARROW
Word right	CTRL+RIGHT ARROW	OPTION+RIGHT ARROW
End of line	END	COMMAND+RIGHT ARROW
Beginning of line	HOME	COMMAND+LEFT ARROW
Paragraph up	CTRL+UP ARROW	OPTION+UP ARROW
Paragraph down	CTRL+DOWN ARROW	OPTION+DOWN ARROW
End of page	CTRL+END	COMMAND+DOWN ARROW
Start of page	CTRL+HOME	COMMAND+UP ARROW
Repeat Find or Go To	SHIFT+F4	COMMAND+F4
To previous object	TAB	COMMAND+UP ARROW
To next object	SHIFT+TAB	OPTION+DOWN ARROW

Outlining

To do this	Windows shortcut	Macintosh shortcut
Promote paragraph	ALT+SHIFT+LEFT ARROW	OPTION+COMMAND+LEFT ARROW
Demote paragraph	ALT+SHIFT+RIGHT ARROW	OPTION+COMMAND+RIGHT ARROW
Move selected paragraphs up	ALT+SHIFT+UP ARROW	OPTION+COMMAND+UP ARROW
Move selected paragraphs down	ALT+SHIFT+DOWN ARROW	OPTION+COMMAND+DOWN ARROW
Show heading level 1	ALT+SHIFT+1	OPTION+SHIFT+1
Expand text under a heading	ALT+SHIFT+PLUS	
Collapse text under a heading	ALT+SHIFT+MINUS	
Show all text and headings	ALT+SHIFT+A	
Display character formatting	Keypad /	Keypad /

Selecting

To do this	Windows shortcut	Macintosh shortcut
Character right	SHIFT+RIGHT ARROW	SHIFT+RIGHT ARROW
Character left	SHIFT+LEFT ARROW	SHIFT+LEFT ARROW
End of word	CTRL+SHIFT+RIGHT ARROW	SHIFT+OPTION+RIGHT ARROW
Beginning of word	CTRL+SHIFT+LEFT ARROW	SHIFT+OPTION+LEFT ARROW
Line up	SHIFT+UP ARROW	SHIFT+UP ARROW
Line down	SHIFT+DOWN ARROW	SHIFT+DOWN ARROW
Select all objects (Slide view)	CTRL+A	COMMAND+A
Select all slides (Slide Sorter view)	CTRL+A	COMMAND+A
Select all text (Outline view)	CTRL+A	COMMAND+A
Select any text	Drag with left mouse button depressed	Drag with mouse button depressed
Select word	Double-click	Double-click
Select paragraph	Triple-click	Triple-click
Drag and drop	Select and drag	Select and drag
Drag and drop copy	CTRL+select and drag	OPTION+select and drag

Windows and Menus

To do this	Windows shortcut	Macintosh shortcut
Go to previous presentation window	CTRL+SHIFT+F6	COMMAND+SHIFT+F6
Go to next presentation window	CTRL+F6	COMMAND+F6
Maximize PowerPoint application window	ALT+F10	
Maximize presentation window	CTRL+F10	
Size presentation window	CTRL+F8	
Restore presentation window to previous size	CTRL+F5	

Menu Commands

File Menu

To use this command	Windows shortcut	Macintosh shortcut
New	CTRL+N	COMMAND+N
Open	CTRL+O	COMMAND+O
Close	CTRL+W or CTRL+F4	COMMAND+W
Save	CTRL+S or SHIFT+F12	COMMAND+S
Save As	F12	F12
Print	CTRL+P or CTRL+SHIFT+F12	COMMAND+P
Exit/Quit	CTRL+Q or ALT+F4	COMMAND+Q

Edit Menu

To use this command	Windows shortcut	Macintosh shortcut
Undo	CTRL+Z	COMMAND+Z
Clear	DELETE	DEL
Cut	CTRL+X	COMMAND+X
Copy	CTRL+C, CTRL+INSERT	COMMAND+C
Paste	CTRL+V, SHIFT+INSERT	COMMAND+V
Select all	CTRL+A	COMMAND+A
Find	CTRL+F	COMMAND+F
Replace	CTRL+H	COMMAND+H
Duplicate	CTRL+D	COMMAND+D

View Menu

To do this	Windows shortcut	Macintosh shortcut
Slide View	CTRL+ALT+N	COMMAND+OPTION+N
Slide Sorter View	CTRL+ALT+P	COMMAND+OPTION+P
Outline View	CTRL+ALT+O	COMMAND+OPTION+O
Show Guides (toggle)	CTRL+G	COMMAND+G
Switch from normal view to master view	SHIFT+click view button	SHIFT+click view button

Insert Menu

To do this	Windows shortcut	Macintosh shortcut
New slide	CTRL+M	COMMAND+M
New slide without AutoLayout dialog	CTRL+SHIFT+M	COMMAND+SHIFT+M
Date	ALT+SHIFT+D	OPTION+SHIFT+D
Page number	ALT+SHIFT+P	OPTION+SHIFT+P
Time	ALT+SHIFT+T	OPTION+SHIFT+T

Format Menu

To do this	Windows shortcut	Macintosh shortcut
Character	CTRL+T	COMMAND+T
Center paragraph	CTRL+E	COMMAND+E
Justified paragraph	CTRL+J	COMMAND+J
Left-aligned paragraph	CTRL+L	COMMAND+L
Right-aligned paragraph	CTRL+R	COMMAND+R

Tools Menu

To do this	Windows shortcut	Macintosh shortcut
Check spelling	CTRL+ALT+L	COMMAND+OPTION+L

Draw Menu

To do this	Windows shortcut	Macintosh shortcut
Restore picture to original size	CTRL+double-click resize handles	OPTION+double-click resize handles
Restore picture to proportional size	SHIFT+double-click resize handles	SHIFT+double-click resize handles
Move from title to text	CTRL+ENTER	OPTION+RETURN
Show title in Slide Sorter	ALT+click	COMMAND+click
Group	CTRL+SHIFT+G	COMMAND+SHIFT+G
Ungroup	CTRL+SHIFT+H	COMMAND+SHIFT+H
Regroup	CTRL+SHIFT+J	COMMAND+SHIFT+J

Help Menu

To do this	Windows shortcut	Macintosh shortcut
Contents	F1	HELP
Context sensitive	SHIFT+F1	SHIFT+HELP

Slide Show

To do this	Windows shortcut	Macintosh shortcut
Go to slide <number>	<Number>+ENTER	<Number>+RETURN
Black/unblack screen	B, . (period)	B, . (period)
White/unwhite screen	W, , (comma)	W, , (comma)
Show/hide pointer	A, =	A, =
Stop/restart automatic show	S, +	S, +
End show	ESC, CTRL+Break, - (minus)	COMMAND+. (period), COMMAND+- (minus), ESC
Erase screen annotations	E	E
Use new time	T	T
Use original time	O	O
Advance on mouse click	M	M
Advance to hidden slide	H	H
Go to slide 1	Hold both mouse buttons down for 2 seconds	Hold both mouse buttons down for 2 seconds
Advance to next slide	Mouse click, SPACEBAR, N, RIGHT ARROW, DOWN ARROW, PAGE DOWN	Mouse click, N, N, RIGHT ARROW, DOWN ARROW, PAGE DOWN
Return to previous slide	Click right mouse button, BACKSPACE, P, LEFT ARROW, UP ARROW, PAGE UP	COMMAND+SHIFT+TAB, DEL, P, LEFT ARROW, UP ARROW, PAGE UP

PowerPoint Toolbars and Tools

PowerPoint Toolbars

Different toolbars appear automatically in each view. For example, the Standard, Formatting, and Drawing toolbars are displayed automatically in Slide view. You can, however, choose to display any toolbar in any view by choosing Toolbars from the View menu, and then selecting the toolbar you want in the Toolbar dialog box. The only exception is the Slide Sorter toolbar, which is available only in Slide Sorter view.

Toolbars are discussed in more detail in the chapters that describe how the tools are applied.

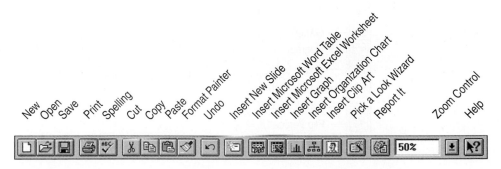

Standard toolbar

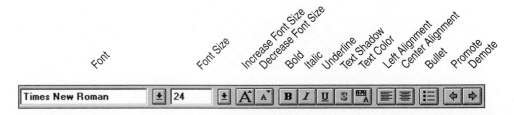

Formatting toolbar

Drawing toolbar

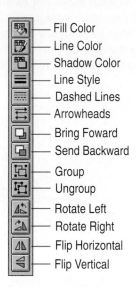

Drawing+ toolbar

Microsoft toolbar

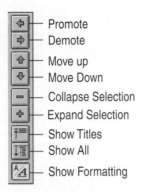

Outlining toolbar

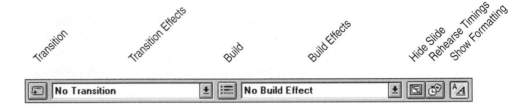

Slide Sorter toolbar

PowerPoint Tools

PowerPoint includes tools that don't appear on any of the toolbars. These tools are stored in the Customize Toolbars dialog box. You can make use of these tools by adding them to any toolbar or by creating a custom toolbar.

PowerPoint Tools in the Customize Toolbars Dialog Box

Tool Name	Tool	Category	Description
Align Bottoms		Arrange	Aligns the bottommost edge of the selected objects
Align Centers		Arrange	Vertically aligns the centers of the selected objects
Align Lefts		Arrange	Aligns the leftmost edge of the selected objects
Align Middles		Arrange	Aligns the centers of the selected objects

Align Rights		Arrange	Aligns the rightmost edge of the selected objects
Align Tops		Arrange	Aligns the topmost edge of the selected objects
Apply Style		Format	Applies the previously picked up attributes to the selection or to defaults
Bring to Front		Arrange	Moves the selection in front of all other objects on the slide
Crop		Tools	Hides portions of the selected picture
Date		Insert	Adds the current date onto the Slide Master
Decrease Paragraph Spacing		Format	Decreases the space between the selected paragraphs
Duplicate		Arrange	Creates a copy of the selection
Find		Edit	Searches the presentation for specified text
Find File		File	Searches for a file by name or other attributes
Guides		Arrange	Shows or hides the drawing guide lines (toggle)
Increase Paragraph Spacing		Format	Increases the space between selected paragraphs
Insert Equation		Insert	Adds an equation onto the slide
Insert Imager		Insert	Inserts a Microsoft Imager object onto the slide
Insert New Slide		Insert	Inserts a new slide after the current slide

Insert Picture		Insert	Adds a picture from a graphics file onto the slide
Insert Sound Object		Insert	Adds a sound object onto the slide
Insert WordArt		Insert	Adds a Microsoft WordArt object onto the slide
Justify		Format	Aligns both left and right edges of each line of text
Microsoft Calculator		Tools	Starts or switches to Microsoft Calculator
Notes Page View		View	Changes the view to edit speaker's notes
Outline View		View	Changes the view to show the title and body text from all slides
Page Numbers		Insert	Adds page numbers onto the Slide Master
Pick Up Style		Format	Picks up the attributes of the selection
Right Alignment		Format	Aligns the right edges of each line of text
Routing Slip		File	Adds or changes the electronic mail routing slip of the active presentation
Send Mail		File	Sends the active presentation through electronic mail
Send to Back		Arrange	Moves the selection behind all other objects on the slide
Slide Master		View	Changes the view to edit objects that appear on every slide
Slide Show		View	Runs or rehearses a slide show with options chosen

Slide Sorter View		View	Changes the view to show miniatures of all slides
Slide View		View	Changes the view to edit a slide
Time		Insert	Adds the current time onto the Slide Master
Zoom Control		View	Changes the scale at which you edit

APPENDIX E

Microsoft Support Services

If you have a question about Microsoft PowerPoint, first look in the PowerPoint User's Guide or consult online Help. You can also find late-breaking updates and technical information in the Readme file that came with your PowerPoint disks. If you cannot find the answer, contact the Microsoft Support Network.

The Microsoft Support Network

The Microsoft Support Network offers you a wide range of choices and access to high-quality, responsive technical support. Microsoft recognizes that support needs vary from user to user; the Microsoft Support Network allows you to choose the type of support that best meets your needs, with options ranging from electronic bulletin boards to annual support programs.

Services vary outside the United States and Canada. In other locations, contact a local Microsoft subsidiary for information. The Microsoft Support Network is subject to Microsoft's then-current prices, terms, and conditions, and is subject to change without notice.

Product Support Within the United States and Canada

In the United States and Canada, the following support services are available through the Microsoft Support Network:

Use the System Info feature to view information about your system

The System Info feature examines your computer and displays information about PowerPoint and your operating system. This information may be useful to the technical support engineer, should you need to call for assistance.

▶ **To see information with the System Info feature**

1. From the Help menu, choose About PowerPoint.

2. Choose the System Info button.

3. In the Choose A Category box, select the type of information you want.

You can also save or print information and run programs from the System Info dialog box.

Electronic Services

These services are available 24 hours a day, 7 days a week, including holidays.

Microsoft FastTips (800) 936-4100 on a touch-tone telephone. Receive automated answers to common questions, and access a library of technical notes, all delivered by recording or fax. You can use the following keys on your touch-tone telephone after you reach FastTips:

To	Press
Advance to the next message	*
Repeat the current message	7
Return to the beginning of FastTips	#

CompuServe Interact with other users and Microsoft support engineers, or access the Microsoft Knowledge Base to get product information. At any ! prompt, type **go microsoft** to access Microsoft forums, or type **go mskb** to access the Microsoft Knowledge Base. For an introductory CompuServe membership kit, call (800) 848-8199, operator 519.

Microsoft Download Service Access, via modem, the Driver Library and the most current technical notes (1200, 2400, or 9600 baud; no parity; 8 data bits; 1 stop bit). In the United States, call (206) 936-6735. In Canada, call (905) 507-3022.

Internet Access the Driver Library and the Microsoft Knowledge Base. The Microsoft Internet FTP archive host, ftp.microsoft.com, supports anonymous login. When logging in as anonymous, you should type your complete electronic mail name as your password.

Standard Support

In the United States, no-charge support from Microsoft support engineers is available via a toll call between 6:00 A.M. and 6:00 P.M. Pacific time, Monday through Friday, excluding holidays.

- For technical support for PowerPoint for Windows, call (206) 635-7145.

- For technical support for PowerPoint for the Macintosh, call (206) 635-7145.

In Canada, support engineers are available via a toll call between 8:00 A.M. and 8:00 P.M. Eastern time, Monday through Friday, excluding holidays. Call (905) 568-3503.

When you call, you should be at your computer and have the appropriate product documentation at hand. Be prepared to give the following information:

- The version number of the Microsoft product that you are using.
- The type of hardware that you are using.
- The exact wording of any messages that appeared on your screen.
- A description of what happened and what you were doing when the problem occurred.
- A description of how you tried to solve the problem.

Priority Support

The Microsoft Support Network offers priority telephone access to Microsoft support engineers 24 hours a day, 7 days a week, except holidays.

- In the United States, call (900) 555-2000; $2 (U.S.) per minute, $25 (U.S.) maximum. Charges appear on your telephone bill. Not available in Canada.
- In the United States, call (800) 936-5700; $25 (U.S.) per incident, billed to your VISA card, MasterCard, or American Express card. In Canada, call (800) 668-7975; $30 per incident, billed to your VISA card, MasterCard, or American Express card.

Text Telephone

Microsoft text telephone (TT/TDD) services are available for the deaf or hard-of-hearing. In the United States, using a TT/TDD modem, dial (206) 635-4948 between 6:00 A.M. and 6:00 P.M. Pacific time, Monday through Friday, excluding holidays. In Canada, using a TT/TDD modem, dial (905) 568-9641 between 8:00 A.M. and 8:00 P.M. Eastern time, Monday through Friday, excluding holidays.

Other Support Options

The Microsoft Support Network offers annual support plans. For information, in the United States, contact the Microsoft Support Network Sales and Information group at (800) 936-3500 between 6:00 A.M. and 6:00 P.M. Pacific time, Monday through Friday, excluding holidays. In Canada, call (800) 668-7975 between 8:00 A.M. and 8:00 P.M. Eastern time, Monday through Friday, excluding holidays.

Product Training and Consultation

Microsoft Solution Providers are independent organizations that provide consulting, integration, customization, development, technical support and training, and other services for Microsoft products. These companies are called Solution Providers because they apply technology and provide services to help solve real-world problems.

In the United States, for more information about the Microsoft Solution Providers program or the Microsoft Solution Provider nearest to you, please call (800) 426-9400 between 6:30 A.M. and 5:30 P.M. Pacific time, Monday through Friday, excluding holidays. In Canada, call (800) 668-7975 between 8:00 A.M. and 8:00 P.M. Eastern time, Monday through Friday, excluding holidays.

Product Support Worldwide

If you are outside the United States and have a question about a Microsoft product, first:

- Consult the documentation and other printed information included with your product.
- Check online Help.
- Check the README files that come with your product disks. These files provide general information that became available after the books in the product package were published.
- Consult electronic options such as CompuServe forums or bulletin boards, if available.

If you cannot find a solution, you can receive information on how to obtain product support by contacting the Microsoft subsidiary office that serves your country.

The Microsoft Support Network

The Microsoft Support Network, where available, offers you a wide range of choices and access to high quality, responsive technical support. Microsoft recognizes that support needs vary from user to user; the Microsoft Support Network allows you to choose the type of support that best meets your needs, with options ranging from electronic bulletin boards to annual support programs.

The Microsoft Support Network is subject to Microsoft's then-current prices, terms, and conditions in place in each country at the time the services are used and is subject to change without notice.

Calling a Microsoft Subsidiary Office

When you call, you should be at your computer and have the appropriate product documentation at hand. Be prepared to give the following information:

- The version number of Microsoft product that you are using.
- The type of hardware that you are using, including network hardware, if applicable.
- The operating system that you are using.

- The exact wording of any messages that appeared on your screen.
- A description of what happened and what you were doing when the problem occurred.
- A description of how you tried to solve the problem.

Microsoft subsidiary offices and the countries they serve are listed below.

If there is no Microsoft office in your country, please contact the establishment from which you purchased your Microsoft product.

Area	Telephone Numbers
Argentina	Microsoft de Argentina S.A. Customer Service: (54) (1) 814-5105 (54) (1) 814-4807 (54) (1) 814-4808 (54) (1) 811-7199 Technical Support: (54) (1) 815-1521 Fax: (54) (1) 814-0372
Australia	Microsoft Pty. Ltd. Install & Setup: (61) (02) 870-2870 Fax: (61) (02) 805-1108 Bulletin Board Service: (61) (02) 870-2348 Technical Support: (61) (02) 870-2131 Sales Information Centre: (61) (02) 870-2100
Belgium	Microsoft NV Phone: 02-7303911 Customer Service: 02-7303922 CompuServe: 02-2150530 (GO MSBEN) Bulletin Board Service: 02-7350045 (1200/2400/9600 baud, 8 bits, no parity, 1 stop bit, ANSI terminal emulation) Technical Support: (Dutch speaking): 02-5133274 (English speaking): 02-5023432 (French speaking): 02-5132268
Bolivia	See Argentina
Brazil	Microsoft Informatica Ltda. Phone: (55) (11) 530-4455 Fax: (55) (11) 240-2205 Technical Support Phone: (55) (11) 533-2922 Technical Support Fax: (55) (11) 241-1157 Technical Support Bulletin Board Service: (55) (11) 65-8564

Canada	Microsoft Canada Inc. Phone: 1 (905) 568-0434 Technical Support Phone: 1 (905) 568-3503 Technical Support Bulletin Board Service: 1 (905) 507-3022 Text Telephone (TT/TDD) 1 (905) 568-9641
Chile	Microsoft Chile S.A. Tel: 56 2 218 5771, 56 2 218 5711, 56 2 218 7524 Fax: 56 2 218 5747
Colombia	Microsoft Colombia Tel: (571) 618 2245 Soporte Tecnico: (571) 618 2255 Fax:(571) 618 2269
Denmark	Microsoft Denmark AS Phone: (45) (44) 89 01 00 Technical Support: (45) (44) 89 01 11 Microsoft Sales Support: (45) (44) 89 01 90 Microsoft BBS: (45) (44) 66 90 46 (Document 303030 in FaxSvar contains detailed instructions) Microsoft FaxSvar: (45) (44) 89 01 44
Dubai	Microsoft Middle East Phone: (971) 4 513 888 Fax: (971) 4 527 444
England	See United Kingdom
Finland	Microsoft OY Phone: (358) (0) 525 501 Phone: (358) (9) 0 525 501 Microsoft BBS: (46) (0) 8 750 47 42 (Information in Swedish and English) Microsoft FaxSvar: (46) (0)8 752 29 00 (Information in Swedish and English)
France	Microsoft France Phone: (33) (1) 69-86-46-46 Telex: MSPARIS 604322F Fax: (33) (1) 64-46-06-60 Technical Support Phone: (33) (1) 69-86-10-20 Technical Support Fax: (33) (1) 69-28-00-28 Fax Information Service (33) (1) 69-29-11-55
French Polynesia	See France
Germany	Microsoft GmbH Phone: 089 - 3176-0 Telex: (17) 89 83 28 MS GMBH D Fax: 089 - 3176-1000 Information: 089 - 3176 1199 Prices, updates, etc.: 089 - 3176 1199 Bulletin board, device drivers, tech notes : Btx: microsoft# or *610808000# CompuServe: GO MSEURO (Microsoft Central Europe) Technical support: 089 3176 1120

Greece	Microsoft Hellas, S.A. Phone: (30) (1) 6893 631 through (30) 1 6893 635 Fax: (30) (1) 6893 636
Hong Kong	Microsoft Hong Kong Limited Technical Support: (852) 804-4222 Fax: (852) 560-2217
Ireland	See United Kingdom
Israel	Microsoft Israel Ltd. Phone: 972-3-575-7034 Fax: 972-3-575-7065
Italy	Microsoft SpA Phone: (39) (2) 269121 Telex: 340321 I Fax: (39) (2) 21072020 Customer Service (Prices, new product info, product literature): (39) (2) 26901359 Bulletin Board: (39) (2) 21072051 Technical Support: (39) (2) 26901363
Japan	Microsoft Company Ltd. Tokyo Japan Phone: (81) (3) 5454-8025 Fax: (81) (3) 5454-7972 PSS Technical Support Fax: (81) (3) 5454-7955 Customer Service Phone (Version upgrade/Registration) Phone: (81) (3) 5454 2305 Fax: (81) (3) 5454-7952 Channel Marketing (Pre-sales Product Support) Information Center Phone: (81) (3) 5454-2300 Fax: (81) (3) 5454 7951
Korea	Microsoft CH Phone: (82) (2) 552-9505 Fax: (82) (2) 555-1724 Technical Support: (82) (2) 563-9230 Technical Support Fax : (82) (2) 563-5194 Technical Support Bulletin Board Service : (82) (2) 538-3256
Liechtenstein	See Switzerland (German speaking)
Luxembourg	Microsoft NV Phone. (32) 2-7303911 Customer Service: (32) 2-7303922 CompuServe: (32) 2-2150530 (GO MSBEN) Bulletin Board Service: (32) 2-7350045 (1200/2400/9600 baud, 8 bits, No parity, 1 stop bit, ANSI terminal emulation) Technical Support: (Dutch speaking): (32) 2-5133274 (English speaking): (32) 2-5023432 (French speaking): (32) 2-5132268

México	Microsoft México, S.A. de C.V. Phone: (52) (5) 325-0910 Customer Service: (52) (5) 325-0911 Desktop & OS: (52) (5) 237-4800 Bulletin Board Service: (52) (5) 590-5988 (1200/2400 baud, 8 bits, No parity, 1 stop bit, ANSI terminal emulation) Fax: (52) (5) 280-7940 Technical Support: (52) (5) 325-0912
Netherlands	Microsoft BV Phone: 02503-89189 Customer Service: 02503-77700 CompuServe: 020-6880085 (GO MSBEN) Bulletin Board Service: 02503-34221 (1200/2400/9600 baud, 8 bits, No parity, 1 stop bit, ANSI terminal emulation) Technical Support: (Dutch speaking) Technical Support: 02503-77877 (English speaking) Technical Support: 02503-77853
New Zealand	Technology Link Centre Phone: 64 (9) 358-3724 Fax: 64 (9) 358-3726 Technical Support Applications: 64 (9) 357-5575
Northern Ireland	See United Kingdom
Norway	Microsoft Norway AS Phone: (47) (22) 18 35 00 Technical Support: (47) (22) 02 25 50 Microsoft Sales Support: (47) 22 02 25 80 Microsoft BBS: (47) 22 18 22 09 (Document 404040 in FaxSvar contains detailed instructions) Microsoft FaxSvar: (47) 22 02 25 70
Papua New Guinea	See Australia
Paraguay	See Argentina
Portugal	MSFT, Lda. Phone: (351) 1 4412205 Fax: (351) 1 4412101
Republic of China	Microsoft Taiwan Corp. Phone: (886) (2) 504-3122 Fax: (886) (2) 504-3121 Technical Support : (886) (2) 508-9501
Republic of Ireland	See United Kingdom
Scotland	See United Kingdom
South Africa	Phone: (27) 11 444 0520 Fax: (27) 11 444 0536

Spain	Microsoft Iberica SRL Phone: (34) (1) 804-0000 Fax: (34) (1) 803-8310 Technical Support: (34) (1) 803-9960
Sweden	Microsoft AB Phone: (46) (8) 752 56 00 Information on Technical Support: (46) (8) 752 09 29 Sales Support: (46) (8) 752 56 30 Microsoft BBS: (46) (8) 750 47 42 (Document 202020 in FaxSvar contains detailed instructions) Microsoft FaxSvar: (46) (0)8 752 29 00
Switzerland	Microsoft AG Phone: 01 - 839 61 11 Fax: 01 - 831 08 69 Documentation: Phone: 155 59 00 Fax: 064 - 224294, Microsoft Info-Service, Postfach, 8099 Zürich Prices, updates, etc.: 01/839 61 11 CompuServe: GO MSEURO(Microsoft Central Europe) Technical support: (German speaking) 01 - 342 - 4082 Technical support: (French speaking) 022 - 738 96 88
Turkey	Microsoft Turkey Phone: (90) 212 2585998 Fax: (90) 212 2585954

United Kingdom	Microsoft Limited
	Phone: (44) (734) 270000
	Fax: (44) (734) 270002
	Upgrades: (44) (81) 614 8000
	Technical Support:
	    Main Line (All Products): (44) (734) 271000
	      Bulletin Board Service: (44) (734) 270065 (2400 Baud)
	      Fax Information Service: (44) (734) 270080

Uruguay	See Argentina
Venezuela	Corporation MS 90 de Venezuela S.A. Technical Support: 58.2.910046, 58.2.910510 Other information: 58.2.910008, 58.2.914739, 58.2.913342 Fax: 58.2.923835
Wales	See United Kingdom

APPENDIX F

Sample Templates

PowerPoint comes with about 150 templates in three template families. The template families are in three directories located within the Template directory. They are:

- Color 35mm slides and on-screen presentations (located in the sldshow directory)
- Black and white overheads (located in the bwovrhd folder)
- Color overheads (located in the clrovrhd folder)

Each design is available to you for 35mm slides or on-screen presentations, black and white overheads, and color overheads.

When you apply a template using the Presentation Template command from the Format menu or by pressing the Template button on the status bar, PowerPoint lists all three of the directories or the last directory in which you looked for a template. Select the template family you want, and then select the template you want to apply. When you select a template, a miniature of the template appears in the Preview box. For details on applying templates, see Chapter 2: "Creating Presentations and Slides".

In the following pages, you'll find pictures of selected templates. The name for each template appears below its picture, with the last letter of the name corresponding to its template type: s represents Slideshow, b represents black and white overheads, c represents color overheads.

Sample Templates: From the SLDSHOW Folder

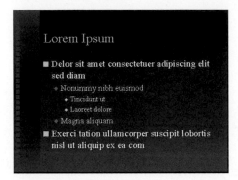

azures.ppt

bevels.ppt

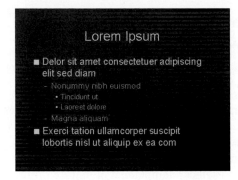

blstrips.ppt

bludiags.ppt

blueboxs.ppt

bluegrns.ppt

checkss.ppt

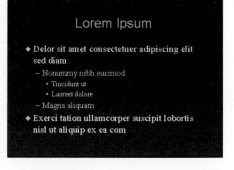

cheerss.ppt

colorbxs.ppt

confetis.ppt

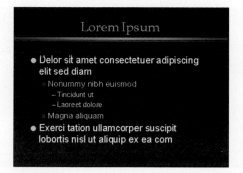

dbllines.ppt

diamonds.ppt

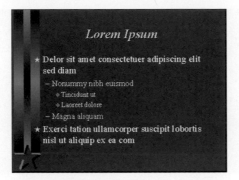

dropstrs.ppt

embossds.ppt

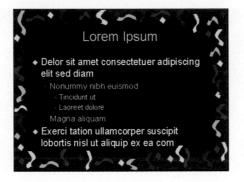

fiestas.ppt

flags.ppt

intls.ppt

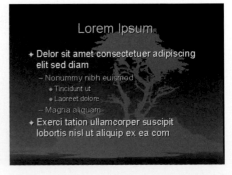

islands.ppt

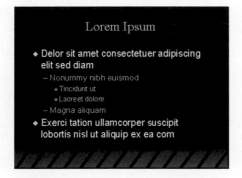

linsblus.ppt

marbles.ppt

medicals.ppt

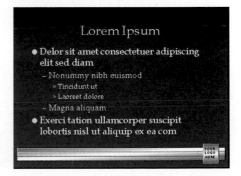

metlbars.ppt

movnglns.ppt

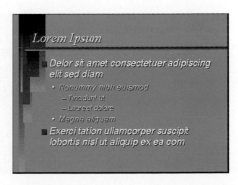

multbars.ppt

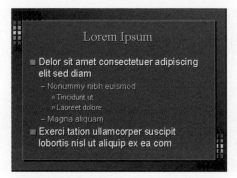

multboxs.ppt

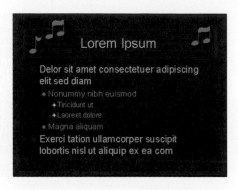

musics.ppt

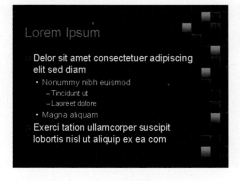

neonlits.ppt

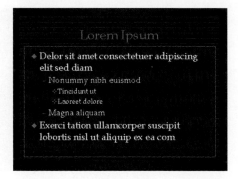

redlines.ppt

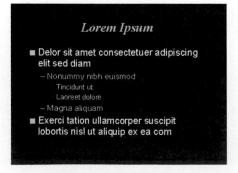

seashors.ppt

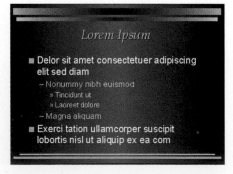

shadbars.ppt

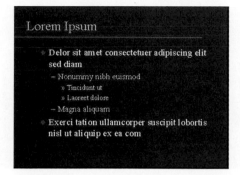

sidebars.ppt

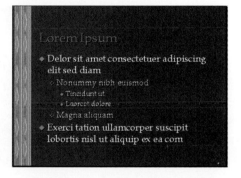

sidefads.ppt

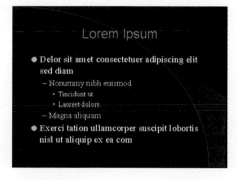

soarings.ppt

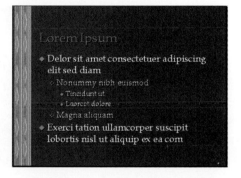

southwss.ppt

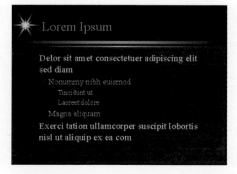

sparkles.ppt

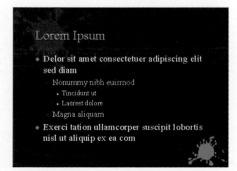

splats.ppt

tablets.ppt

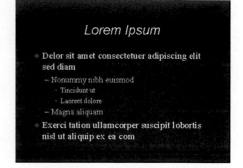

theatres.ppt

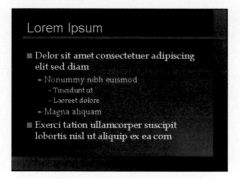

toplines.ppt

travels.ppt

triumphs.ppt

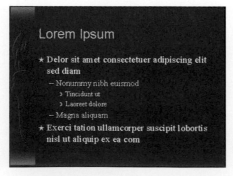

twinkles.ppt

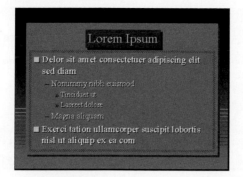

vividlns.ppt

worlds.ppt

Sample Templates: From the CLROVRHD Folder

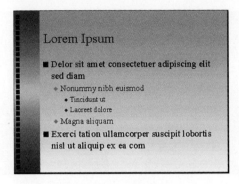

azurec.ppt   **bevelc.ppt**

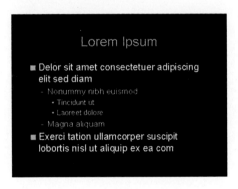

blstripc.ppt   **bludiagc.ppt**

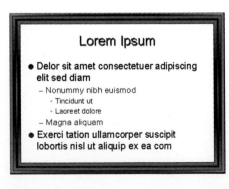

blueboxc.ppt   **bluegrnc.ppt**

Lorem Ipsum

- Delor sit amet consectetuer adipiscing elit sed diam
  - Nonummy nibh euismod
    - Tincidunt ut
    - Laoreet dolore
  - Magna aliquam
- Exerci tation ullamcorper suscipit lobortis nisl ut aliquip ex ea com

checksc.ppt

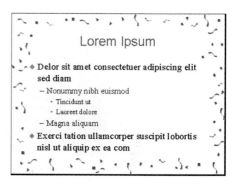

Lorem Ipsum

- Delor sit amet consectetuer adipiscing elit sed diam
  - Nonummy nibh euismod
    - Tincidunt ut
    - Laoreet dolore
  - Magna aliquam
- Exerci tation ullamcorper suscipit lobortis nisl ut aliquip ex ea com

cheersc.ppt

Lorem Ipsum

- Delor sit amet consectetuer adipiscing elit sed diam
  - Nonummy nibh euismod
    - Tincidunt ut
    - Laoreet dolore
  - Magna aliquam
- Exerci tation ullamcorper suscipit lobortis nisl ut aliquip ex ea com

colorbxc.ppt

Lorem Ipsum

- *Delor sit amet consectetuer adipiscing elit sed diam*
  - *Nonummy nibh euismod*
    - *Tincidunt ut*
    - *Laoreet dolore*
  - *Magna aliquam*
- *Exerci tation ullamcorper suscipit lobortis nisl ut aliquip ex ea com*

confetic.ppt

Lorem Ipsum

- Delor sit amet consectetuer adipiscing elit sed diam
  - Nonummy nibh euismod
    - Tincidunt ut
    - Laoreet dolore
  - Magna aliquam
- Exerci tation ullamcorper suscipit lobortis nisl ut aliquip ex ea com

dbllinec.ppt

Lorem Ipsum

- Delor sit amet consectetuer adipiscing elit sed diam
  - Nonummy nibh euismod
    - Tincidunt ut
    - Laoreet dolore
  - Magna aliquam
- Exerci tation ullamcorper suscipit lobortis nisl ut aliquip ex ea com

diamondc.ppt

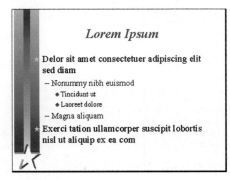

dropstrc.ppt

embossdc.ppt

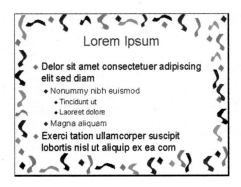

fiestac.ppt

flagc.ppt

intlc.ppt

islandc.ppt

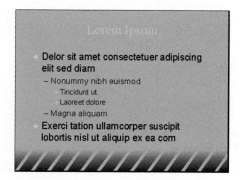

linsbluc.ppt

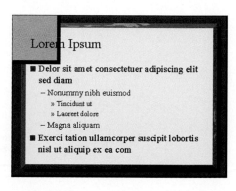

marblec.ppt

medicalc.ppt

metlbarc.ppt

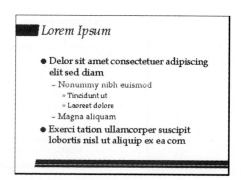

movnglnc.ppt

multbarc.ppt

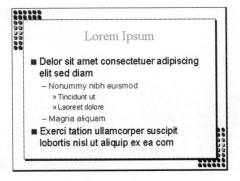

multboxc.ppt

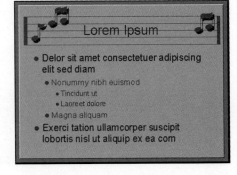

musicc.ppt

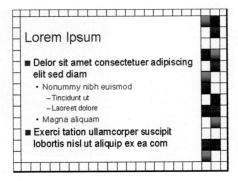

neonlitc.ppt

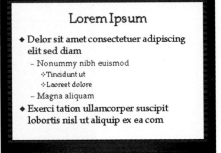

redlinec.ppt

seashorc.ppt

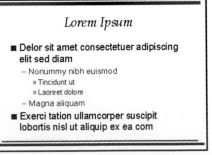

shadbarc.ppt

Lorem Ipsum

- ◆ Delor sit amet consectetuer adipiscing elit sed diam
  - − Nonummy nibh euismod
    - » Tincidunt ut
    - » Laoreet dolore
  - − Magna aliquam
- ◆ Exerci tation ullamcorper suscipit lobortis nisl ut aliquip ex ea com

sidebarc.ppt

Lorem Ipsum

- ■ Delor sit amet consectetuer adipiscing elit sed diam
  - − Nonummy nibh euismod
    - ✧ Tincidunt ut
    - ✧ Laoreet dolore
  - − Magna aliquam
- Exerci tation ullamcorper suscipit lobortis nisl ut aliquip ex ea com

sidefadc.ppt

Lorem Ipsum

- ● Delor sit amet consectetuer adipiscing elit sed diam
  - − Nonummy nibh euismod
    - ● Tincidunt ut
    - ● Laoreet dolore
  - − Magna aliquam
- ● Exerci tation ullamcorper suscipit lobortis nisl ut aliquip ex ea com

soaringc.ppt

Lorem Ipsum

- ◆ Delor sit amet consectetuer adipiscing elit sed diam
  - ✧ Nonummy nibh euismod
    - ● Tincidunt ut
    - ● Laoreet dolore
  - ✧ Magna aliquam
- ● Exerci tation ullamcorper suscipit lobortis nisl ut aliquip ex ea com

southwsc.ppt

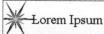

Lorem Ipsum

- ➤ Delor sit amet consectetuer adipiscing elit sed diam
  - ➤ Nonummy nibh euismod
    - ➤ Tincidunt ut
    - ➤ Laoreet dolore
  - ➤ Magna aliquam
- ➤ Exerci tation ullamcorper suscipit lobortis nisl ut aliquip ex ea com

sparklec.ppt

Lorem Ipsum

- ◆ Delor sit amet consectetuer adipiscing elit sed diam
  - ◆ Nonummy nibh euismod
    - ◆ Tincidunt ut
    - ◆ Laoreet dolore
  - ◆ Magna aliquam
- ◆ Exerci tation ullamcorper suscipit lobortis nisl ut aliquip ex ea com

splatc.ppt

tabletc.ppt

Lorem Ipsum

■ Delor sit amet consectetuer adipiscing elit sed diam
  – Nonummy nibh euismod
    • Tincidunt ut
    • Laoreet dolore
  – Magna aliquam
■ Exerci tation ullamcorper suscipit lobortis nisl ut aliquip ex ea com

theatrec.ppt

Lorem Ipsum

◆ Delor sit amet consectetuer adipiscing elit sed diam
  ❖ Nonummy nibh euismod
    ◆ Tincidunt ut
    ◆ Laoreet dolore
  ❖ Magna aliquam
◆ Exerci tation ullamcorper suscipit lobortis nisl ut aliquip ex ea com

toplinec.ppt

Lorem Ipsum

■ Delor sit amet consectetuer adipiscing elit sed diam
  ➤ Nonummy nibh euismod
    – Tincidunt ut
    – Laoreet dolore
  ➤ Magna aliquam
■ Exerci tation ullamcorper suscipit lobortis nisl ut aliquip ex ea com

travelc.ppt

Lorem Ipsum

◆ Delor sit amet consectetuer adipiscing elit sed diam
  – Nonummy nibh euismod
    • Tincidunt ut
    • Laoreet dolore
  – Magna aliquam
◆ Exerci tation ullamcorper suscipit lobortis nisl ut aliquip ex ea com

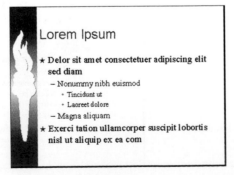

triumphc.ppt

Lorem Ipsum

★ Delor sit amet consectetuer adipiscing elit sed diam
  – Nonummy nibh euismod
    • Tincidunt ut
    • Laoreet dolore
  – Magna aliquam
★ Exerci tation ullamcorper suscipit lobortis nisl ut aliquip ex ea com

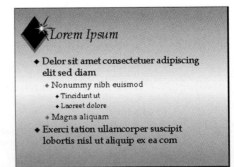

twinklec.ppt

Lorem Ipsum

◆ Delor sit amet consectetuer adipiscing elit sed diam
  ◆ Nonummy nibh euismod
    ◆ Tincidunt ut
    ◆ Laoreet dolore
  ◆ Magna aliquam
◆ Exerci tation ullamcorper suscipit lobortis nisl ut aliquip ex ea com

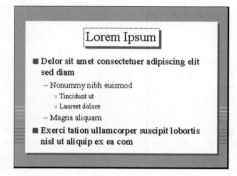

vividlnc.ppt   worldc.ppt

Sample Templates: From BWOVRHD Folder

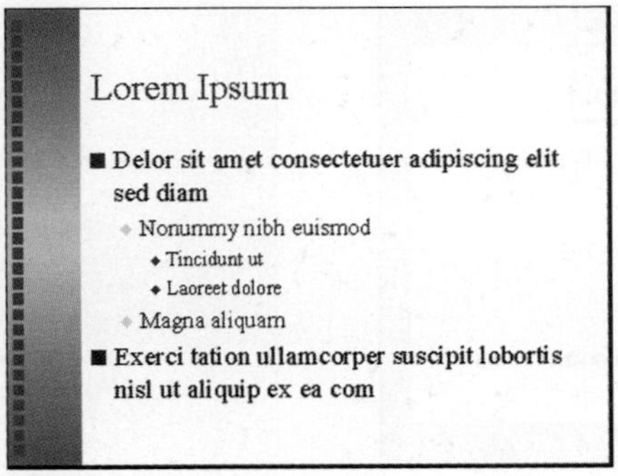

azureb.ppt

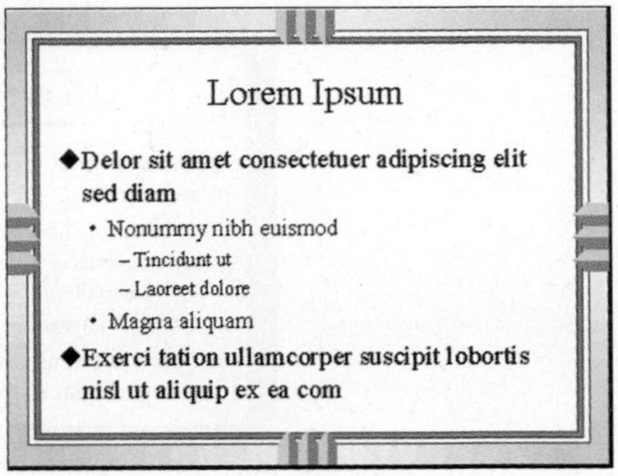

bevelb.ppt

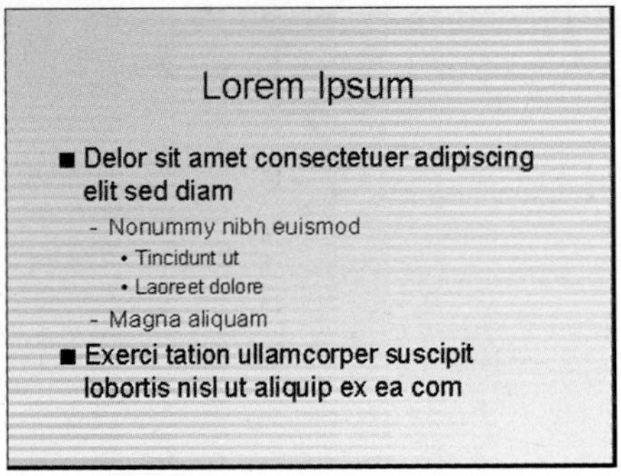

blstripb.ppt

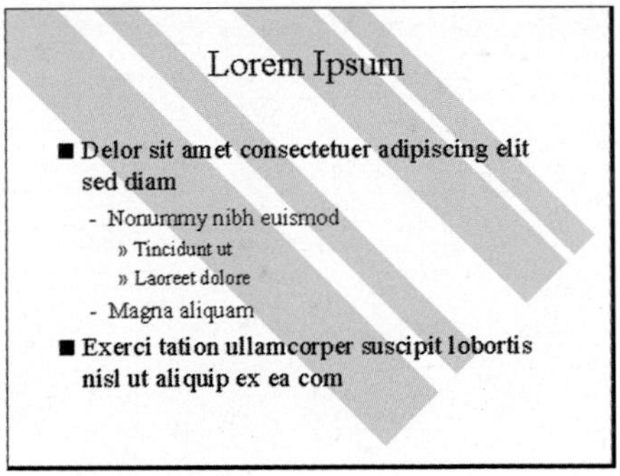

bludiagb.ppt

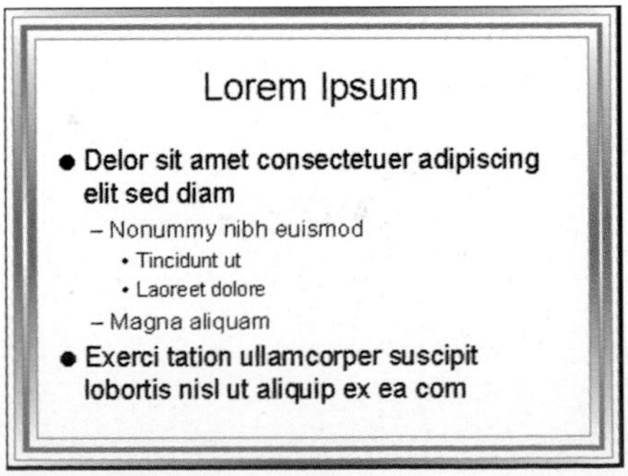

blueboxb.ppt

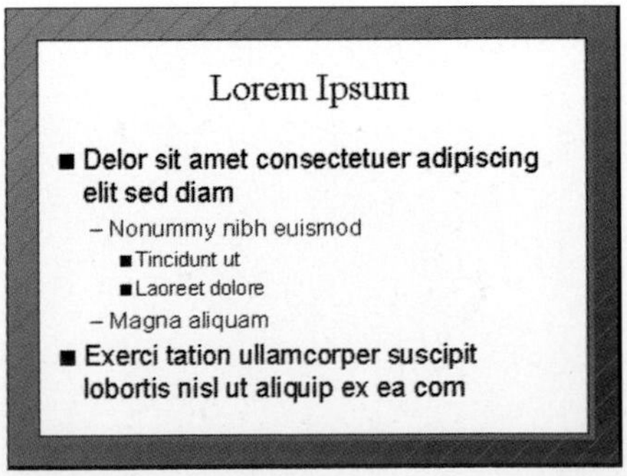

bluegrnb.ppt

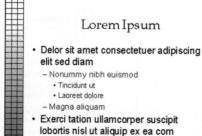

checksb.ppt

cheersb.ppt

colorbxb.ppt

confetib.ppt

dbllineb.ppt

diamondb.ppt

Lorem Ipsum

★ Delor sit amet consectetuer adipiscing elit
 sed diam
 – Nonummy nibh euismod
   ◆ Tincidunt ut
   ◆ Laoreet dolore
 – Magna aliquam
★ Exerci tation ullamcorper suscipit lobortis
 nisl ut aliquip ex ea com

dropstrb.ppt

Lorem Ipsum

■ Delor sit amet consectetuer adipiscing elit
 sed diam
 – Nonummy nibh euismod
   » Tincidunt ut
   » Laoreet dolore
 – Magna aliquam
■ Exerci tation ullamcorper suscipit lobortis
 nisl ut aliquip ex ea com

embossdb.ppt

Lorem Ipsum

◆ Delor sit amet consectetuer adipiscing
 elit sed diam
 ◆ Nonummy nibh euismod
   ◆ Tincidunt ut
   ◆ Laoreet dolore
 ◆ Magna aliquam
◆ Exerci tation ullamcorper suscipit
 lobortis nisl ut aliquip ex ea com

fiestab.ppt

Lorem Ipsum

◆ *Delor sit amet consectetuer adipiscing*
 elit sed diam
 – *Nonummy nibh euismod*
   ✦ *Tincidunt ut*
   ✦ *Laoreet dolore*
 – *Magna aliquam*
◆ *Exerci tation ullamcorper suscipit*
 lobortis nisl ut aliquip ex ea com

flagb.ppt

Lorem Ipsum

✦ Delor sit amet consectetuer adipiscing elit
 sed diam
 – Nonummy nibh euismod
   ◆ Tincidunt ut
   ◆ Laoreet dolore
 – Magna aliquam
✦ Exerci tation ullamcorper suscipit lobortis
 nisl ut aliquip ex ea com

intlb.ppt

Lorem Ipsum

✦ Delor sit amet consectetuer adipiscing
 elit sed diam
 – Nonummy nibh euismod
   ● Tincidunt ut
   ● Laoreet dolore
 – Magna aliquam
✦ Exerci tation ullamcorper suscipit
 lobortis nisl ut aliquip ex ea com

islandb.ppt

Lorem Ipsum

- Delor sit amet consectetuer adipiscing elit sed diam
  - Nonummy nibh euismod
    - Tincidunt ut
    - Laoreet dolore
  - Magna aliquam
- Exerci tation ullamcorper suscipit lobortis nisl ut aliquip ex ea com

linsblub.ppt

Lorem Ipsum

- Delor sit amet consectetuer adipiscing elit sed diam
  - Nonummy nibh euismod
    - Tincidunt ut
    - Laoreet dolore
  - Magna aliquam
- Exerci tation ullamcorper suscipit lobortis nisl ut aliquip ex ea com

marbleb.ppt

Lorem Ipsum

- Delor sit amet consectetuer adipiscing elit sed diam
  - Nonummy nibh euismod
    - Tincidunt ut
    - Laoreet dolore
  - Magna aliquam
- Exerci tation ullamcorper suscipit lobortis nisl ut aliquip ex ea com

medicalb.ppt

Lorem Ipsum

- Delor sit amet consectetuer adipiscing elit sed diam
  - Nonummy nibh euismod
    - Tincidunt ut
    - Laoreet dolore
  - Magna aliquam
- Exerci tation ullamcorper suscipit lobortis nisl ut aliquip ex ea com

metlbarb.ppt

Lorem Ipsum

- Delor sit amet consectetuer adipiscing elit sed diam
  - Nonummy nibh euismod
    - Tincidunt ut
    - Laoreet dolore
  - Magna aliquam
- Exerci tation ullamcorper suscipit lobortis nisl ut aliquip ex ea com

movnglnb.ppt

Lorem Ipsum

- *Delor sit amet consectetuer adipiscing elit sed diam*
  - *Nonummy nibh euismod*
    - *Tincidunt ut*
    - *Laoreet dolore*
  - *Magna aliquam*
- *Exerci tation ullamcorper suscipit lobortis nisl ut aliquip ex ea com*

multbarb.ppt

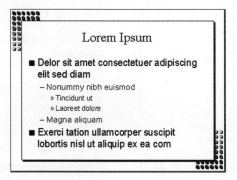

multboxb.ppt

musicb.ppt

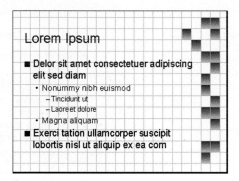

neonlitb.ppt

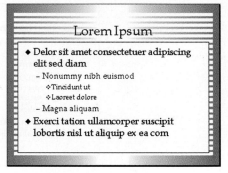

redlineb.ppt

seashorb.ppt

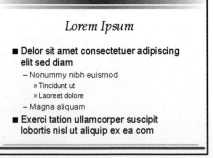

shadbarb.ppt

Lorem Ipsum

- Delor sit amet consectetuer adipiscing elit sed diam
  - Nonummy nibh euismod
    » Tincidunt ut
    » Laoreet dolore
  - Magna aliquam
- Exerci tation ullamcorper suscipit lobortis nisl ut aliquip ex ea com

sidebarb.ppt

Lorem Ipsum

- Delor sit amet consectetuer adipiscing elit sed diam
  - Nonummy nibh euismod
    ✧ Tincidunt ut
    ✧ Laoreet dolore
  - Magna aliquam
- Exerci tation ullamcorper suscipit lobortis nisl ut aliquip ex ea com

sidefadb.ppt

Lorem Ipsum

- Delor sit amet consectetuer adipiscing elit sed diam
  - Nonummy nibh euismod
    • Tincidunt ut
    • Laoreet dolore
  - Magna aliquam
- Exerci tation ullamcorper suscipit lobortis nisl ut aliquip ex ea com

soaringb.ppt

Lorem Ipsum

- Delor sit amet consectetuer adipiscing elit sed diam
  - Nonummy nibh euismod
    • Tincidunt ut
    • Laoreet dolore
  - Magna aliquam
- Exerci tation ullamcorper suscipit lobortis nisl ut aliquip ex ea com

southwsb.ppt

Lorem Ipsum

- Delor sit amet consectetuer adipiscing elit sed diam
  - Nonummy nibh euismod
    ‣ Tincidunt ut
    ‣ Laoreet dolore
  - Magna aliquam
- Exerci tation ullamcorper suscipit lobortis nisl ut aliquip ex ea com

sparkleb.ppt

Lorem Ipsum

- Delor sit amet consectetuer adipiscing elit sed diam
  - Nonummy nibh euismod
    • Tincidunt ut
    • Laoreet dolore
  - Magna aliquam
- Exerci tation ullamcorper suscipit lobortis nisl ut aliquip ex ea com

splatb.ppt

Lorem Ipsum

■ Delor sit amet consectetuer adipiscing elit sed diam
  – Nonummy nibh euismod
    • Tincidunt ut
    • Laoreet dolore
  – Magna aliquam
■ Exerci tation ullamcorper suscipit lobortis nisl ut aliquip ex ea com

tabletb.ppt

Lorem Ipsum

♦ Delor sit amet consectetuer adipiscing elit sed diam
  ❖ Nonummy nibh euismod
    ♦ Tincidunt ut
    ♦ Laoreet dolore
  ❖ Magna aliquam
♦ Exerci tation ullamcorper suscipit lobortis nisl ut aliquip ex ea com

theatreb.ppt

Lorem Ipsum

■ Delor sit amet consectetuer adipiscing elit sed diam
  ➤ Nonummy nibh euismod
    – Tincidunt ut
    – Laoreet dolore
  ➤ Magna aliquam
■ Exerci tation ullamcorper suscipit lobortis nisl ut aliquip ex ea com

toplineb.ppt

Lorem Ipsum

♦ Delor sit amet consectetuer adipiscing elit sed diam
  – Nonummy nibh euismod
    • Tincidunt ut
    • Laoreet dolore
  – Magna aliquam
♦ Exerci tation ullamcorper suscipit lobortis nisl ut aliquip ex ea com

travelb.ppt

Lorem Ipsum

★ Delor sit amet consectetuer adipiscing elit sed diam
  – Nonummy nibh euismod
    • Tincidunt ut
    • Laoreet dolore
  – Magna aliquam
★ Exerci tation ullamcorper suscipit lobortis nisl ut aliquip ex ea com

triumphb.ppt

Lorem Ipsum

♦ Delor sit amet consectetuer adipiscing elit sed diam
  ♦ Nonummy nibh euismod
    ♦ Tincidunt ut
    ♦ Laoreet dolore
  ♦ Magna aliquam
♦ Exerci tation ullamcorper suscipit lobortis nisl ut aliquip ex ea com

twinkleb.ppt

vividlnb.ppt

worldb.ppt

Genigraphics Color Palette

This palette shows the 90 most popular Genigraphics color selections available for visuals prepared in Microsoft PowerPoint. Columns represent the color spectrum. Rows represent different intensities, or shades for each hue selection, ranging from darkest (Row 1) to lightest (Row 7). The colors in Row 8 are saturated (pure) colors. The same palette is shown here on both light and black backgrounds to help you judge the effect your color choices will have in different settings.

Specify colors in PowerPoint using the column name and row number. For instance, YO3 selects a medium-dark shade of Yellow-Orange. Rows 2 and 3 are often used for backgrounds; Rows 6 and 7 are often used for text and headlines.

Note: Due to inherent differences between colors produced by shining light through film and colors produced by 4-color process printing, this chart provides a close approximation of the colors you'll see in your presentations.

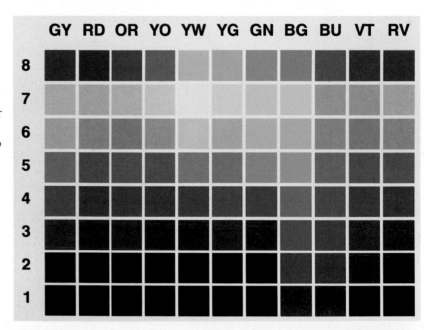

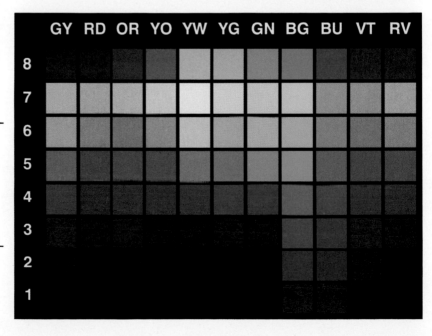

Index

This index includes special *See* and *See also* cross-references to Microsoft PowerPoint online Help keywords. These cross-references are enclosed in quotation marks and follow the word "Help". By searching on these keywords in online Help, you can access additional information on the topics indicated.

SYMBOLS

NUMERALS

A

D

M